MW00985915

A STUDY IN PSALMS

ENCOUNTERING**GOD**

A STUDY IN PSALMS

ENCOUNTERING**GOD**

STEVE PETTIT

journeyforth®

Greenville, South Carolina

The fact that materials produced by other publishers may be referred to in this volume does not constitute an endorsement of the content or theological position of materials produced by such publishers.

All Scripture is quoted from the King James Version.
Photo credits: Steve Pettit ©2016, Hal Cook, BJU Marketing Communications

Authors: Steve Pettit and Eric Newton
Designer: Olivia Hollis
Page layout: Michael Boone

© 2018 by BJU Press
Greenville, South Carolina 29609
JourneyForth Books is a division of BJU Press.

Printed in the United States of America
All rights reserved

ISBN 978-1-62856-488-4
eISBN 978-1-62856-489-1

15   14   13   12   11   10   9   8   7   6   5   4   3   2   1

Contents

KEY

Personal Application

Group Discussion

Cross Reference

New Testament Link

Study Exercise

01

INTRODUCTION TO PSALMS

> The book of Psalms is God's prescription for a complacent church, because through it he reveals how great, wonderful, magnificent, wise, and utterly awe-inspiring he is![1]

Almost everyone has either heard of or read a portion of Psalms. In a ranking of the most popular books in the Bible, Psalms is always number one. So what makes Psalms so engaging? Tremper Longman III writes:

> The Psalms appeal to the whole person; . . . [they] inform our intellect, arouse our emotions, direct our wills and stimulate our imaginations. When we read the Psalms with faith, we come away changed.[2]

Through the Psalms, saints and sinners have experienced a life-changing encounter with God. Moses heard the divine voice speaking out of a burning bush in a lonely spot of the Sinai desert. What was the prophet's response? He took off his shoes and worshiped God. Psalms was written so that we could nurture a similar heart of worship for God.

---

[1]Tremper Longman III and David E. Garland, *The Expositor's Bible Commentary: Psalms* (Grand Rapids: Zondervan, 2008), 23.

[2]Tremper Longman III, *How to Read the Psalms* (Downers Grove: InterVarsity Press, 1988), 13.

> The psalms illuminate the mind for the purpose of enkindling the soul, indeed to put it on fire. It may indeed be said that the purpose of the psalms is to turn the soul into a sort of a burning bush.[3]

We can see the significance of the book of Psalms in the writings of Augustine, the early church father. In his autobiography, *Confessions*, Augustine quotes Psalms on nearly every page. He saw it as central to the reorientation of his life, both morally and spiritually. He spoke of being "set on fire"[4] as he read the book of Psalms. Most strikingly, he viewed a psalm as a narrative of the human soul. It's as if God were narrating the story of Augustine's own heart in Psalms. In Psalms we see both who we are and who God is. We encounter God in our souls.

Who would know this better than the primary author of Psalms, David, whom Samuel described as a "man after his [God's] own heart" (1 Sam. 13:14; Acts 13:22)? In his psalms David draws from various life experiences to express his encounters with the living God through worship. This is the purpose of our study—to encounter God through Psalms.

As we read the book of Psalms, we are entering into the sanctuary, the place where God meets men and women in a special way. So as we begin this journey of encountering God through Psalms, let's consider some of the important elements.

The Book of Psalms: Special Features

- Psalms is the longest book in the Bible (KJV) with 2,461 verses.
- Psalm 119 is the longest chapter in the Bible, containing 176 verses.

---

[3]Stanley L. Jaki, *Praying the Psalms* (Grand Rapids: Eerdmans Publishing Company, 2001), 27.

[4]St. Augustine, *St. Augustine on the Psalms*, eds. Johannes Quasten and Walter J. Burghardt (Mahwah, NJ: Paulist Press, 1960), 91.

- Psalm 117 is the shortest chapter in the Bible, containing only two verses.
- Psalm 117 is also the middle chapter of the Bible, the very center of the 1,189 chapters found in Genesis through Revelation.
- Psalms has more authors than any other book in the Bible. David, the second king of Israel and "sweet psalmist of Israel" (2 Sam. 23:1), is the chief author of Psalms. He is credited with writing 73 of the 150 psalms.
- Psalms took longer to write than any other book of the Bible, from approximately nine hundred to one thousand years (from the fifteenth to the fifth century BC).
- Moses composed the first psalm (Ps. 90) during Israel's forty years of wilderness wanderings (1445–1405 BC). The last psalm composed (Ps. 126) is thought to have been written after the time of the Babylonian exile, during the Jews' return to the land of Judah (between 500 and 430 BC).
- Psalms is the Old Testament book most quoted in the New Testament. Of the 360 Old Testament quotations or allusions in the New Testament, 112 are from Psalms.
- Psalms contains more prophecies concerning the Messiah than any other Old Testament book. They reveal the Messiah, for example, as the Son of God (Ps. 2:7–9) and Son of Man (Ps. 8:5–8) in His obedience (Ps. 40:6–8), betrayal (Ps. 41:9), crucifixion (Ps. 22), resurrection (Ps. 16:10–11), ascension (Ps. 68:18), and enthronement (Ps. 110:1–4).
- Psalms was the Jewish song book. The Hebrew word for *psalms* means *praises*. The Greek word means *the plucking of strings*. The psalms are praise songs to be sung to the musical accompaniment of a plucked or stringed instrument such as a harp or lyre. The collection of these 150 psalms into one book served as the

first hymnbook for God's people, written and compiled to assist them in their worship of God.

 Take some time to read Psalm 2 and then Acts 4:23–31, which quotes this psalm. What do you notice about the early Christians' application of Psalm 2?

_____

_____

_____

_____

_____

The Book of Psalms: Style

The psalms are Hebrew poetry, which is very different from standard English forms of poetry that are based on rhyme and meter. Hebrew poetry is based on rhythm and parallelism. The most basic verse form is two lines. The first line states an idea, and the second line reinforces that idea somehow.

- The second line may restate the first. This is known as *synonymous parallelism.*
- The second line may contrast with the first. This is known as *antithetic parallelism.*
- The second line may build on the first. This is known as *climactic parallelism.*

Read Psalm 6 and identify the verses that use synonymous parallelism.

_____

_____

_____

Hebrew poetry creates vivid pictures that stir up one's emotions. One clear example of this is Psalm 23, the beloved psalm about our Shepherd.

What colorful word pictures are expressed in Psalm 23?

Though all psalms are songs of worship, their purposes and content vary. We cannot be dogmatic about the different types, but the following list is helpful.[5]

1. Wisdom psalms
   These psalms point believers to live godly lives by making right choices in the pursuit of God's will. (For example, Pss. 1, 37, and 119)

2. Lament psalms
   The lament is the emotional heart cry of the psalmist who is living in distressing and difficult times and turns to God for deliverance. (For example, Pss. 22, 42–43, 51, and 102)

3. Royal or Kingship psalms
   These are psalms that prophesy of the coming rule of Jesus as the Messiah. Christ is seen as the coming sovereign ruler. (For example, Pss. 2, 18, 45, 72, 89, 110, and 132)

[5] Longman, *How to Read the Psalms,* 23–34.

4. Thanksgiving psalms
   These psalms express gratitude for God's abundant blessings, whether they are from an individual or from the nation. (For example, Pss. 33, 34, 66, 103, and 146–150)

5. Remembrance psalms
   God's redemption through history is the center of attention in the remembrance psalms. In such psalms, a series of God's acts will be recounted. (For example, Pss. 78, 105, 106, 135, and 136)

6. Confidence psalms
   The psalmist acknowledges his trust and reliance in God's protection, power, and provision. He is able to be at peace because he has confidence in God. (For example, Pss. 16, 23, 62, 91, and 121)

The Book of Psalms: Superscriptions

One hundred sixteen of the psalms have titles, headings, or notations at the beginning. These serve to identify the author, to establish the historical circumstances and context, or to explain how the psalm should be sung or played on a variety of musical instruments. These superscriptions assisted the worship leader and the congregation to sing the psalms knowledgeably. The superscriptions are considered to be a part of the author's original composition.

One other notable designation is the word *Selah*. It is found seventy-one times in Psalms. The meaning is debatable. It could be a signal for either a change of musical accompaniment, a brief interlude with stringed instruments, a notice to begin a new section, or a call to pause and reflect upon the truth just stated. This final possibility is still a healthy habit today. We need to stop and reflect on the truths of Psalms.

So how do we encounter God in Psalms? What are some of the key steps we can take in worshiping God through Psalms?

Meditate

Meditation is the act of thinking or mulling over the truth of the Scripture. Meditation begins by reading the text. Take time to read the psalm of the week every day. Write down your observations. This is called journaling. Make a biography of God. Look at how God reveals Himself in the text of the Scripture. Focus your attention on God's character. Memorize the verses of the psalm that speak directly to you and inspire your faith.

> Augustine spent an hour of every day for several decades meditating on the Book of Psalms verse by verse. In this fashion he put into writing his reflections on the psalms.[6]

Pray

Let the book of Psalms be your prayer guide. It is a series of prayers. Since the meaning of the Hebrew name for *psalms* is *praise*, reading the psalms should stir us to praise God. Here is a brief example of praying the psalms:

> "Make a joyful noise unto the Lord, all ye lands." (Ps. 100:1)

> *Father, I rejoice today in You. May Your name be praised and worshiped throughout the world.*

> "Serve the Lord with gladness." (Ps. 100:2)

> *Lord, please accept my service in a way that will please You. Thank You for the opportunity You have given me to serve. I love You and am so happy in what You have given me to do.*

---

[6]William D. Barrick, "Psalms, Hymns, and Spiritual Songs: The Master Musician's Melodies," 2008, http://drbarrick.org/files/studynotes/Psalms/Pss_Intro_rev.pdf.

7

Put this emphasis into practice by praying Psalm 100:3 and 100:5.

_____

_____

_____

_____

_____

Sing

The book of Psalms was both the Jewish prayer book and song book. By singing we engage our emotions in the truth of the psalms. Singing is the culmination of encountering God in the psalms after we meditate on and pray these inspired songs.

Notes

02

PSALM 1
DISCOVERING TRUE HAPPINESS

The great test of man is his relationship to the "law of
the Lord." The godly man accepts it. The ungodly man
spurns it.[1]

Psalm 1 is called the preamble to the book of Psalms. That
is, it serves as an introduction to the entire book. What is
said in Psalm 1 is relevant to all the rest of the book of Psalms.
Charles Spurgeon viewed it this way:

> The matter of the first Psalm, which may be looked
> upon, in some respects, as the text upon which the
> whole of the Psalms make up a divine sermon.[2]

The psalms begin with these words: "Blessed is the man." In
Psalm 1, God addresses man's most basic question: How can I
be happy (blessed) in this life?

Is this true? Does God really want us to be happy? Absolutely!
And this happiness is not temporary, but perpetual. The word
translated *blessed* is plural in the original Hebrew. That is,

---

[1]Peter A. Steveson, *Psalms* (Greenville, SC: Bob Jones University Press,
2007), 3.
[2]C. H. Spurgeon, *The Treasury of David* (Peabody, MA: Hendrickson
Publishers, 1988), 1:1.

it means perpetual blessings. It can be read *blessednesses* or *happinesses.*

So how can I be happy, truly happy? Psalm 1 is called a wisdom psalm because we learn that happiness results from our choice to follow God's direction of life. In this psalm the writer sets forth two ways or two directions in life. One is the right way that leads to happiness, and the other is the wrong way that leads to misery.

What are the most common ways people seek happiness today? Why?

The Right Way

Psalm 1:1–3

Blessed is the man that walketh not in the counsel of the ungodly, nor standeth in the way of sinners, nor sitteth in the seat of the scornful. But his delight is in the law of the Lord; and in his law doth he meditate day and night. And he shall be like a tree planted by the rivers of water, that bringeth forth his fruit in his season; his leaf also shall not wither; and whatsoever he doeth shall prosper.

Psalm 1 captures a fundamental teaching found in both the Old and New Testaments. In the Old Testament God teaches His people that one's choice will determine both the direction and the outcome of your life.

> I call heaven and earth to record this day against
> you, that I have set before you life and death, bless-
> ing and cursing: therefore choose life, that both
> thou and thy seed may live. (Deut. 30:19)

In the New Testament, Jesus' message to the crowds is to choose the right way in life:

> Enter ye in at the strait gate: for wide is the gate,
> and broad is the way, that leadeth to destruction,
> and many there be which go in thereat: because
> strait is the gate, and narrow is the way, which lead-
> eth unto life, and few there be that find it. (Matt.
> 7:13–14)

Choosing the Right Path

First, in Psalm 1:1 we learn that happiness comes by choos-ing to walk on a righteous path. This determination is directly connected to other people. Each line in this verse tells us to avoid the wrong kinds of interpersonal relationships. Your friends make all the difference in your life.

Notice what the verse says: "Blessed is the man that walketh not in the counsel of the ungodly." Choosing the righteous path includes refusing advice from those who hold godless values and whose moral choices violate the laws of God.

The second line goes a step further: "nor standeth in the way of sinners." It is one thing to listen to wicked counsel. It is an-other to decisively side with that viewpoint. Instead, the happy person refuses to follow the worldly crowd. You don't see him "hanging out" with those who pursue sin as a lifestyle.

Finally, he refuses to sit and associate with those whose con-versations mock and curse God: "nor sitteth in the seat of the scornful." If you want to be miserable, make your best friends those who are scornful, critical, and disrespectful.

The three verbs—*walk*, *stand*, and *sit*—show the slippery slope of evil. Evil is not passive. It is ever descending. The longer you go, the worse you get. A pattern of evil choices causes a downward spiral in character that leads to destruction.

The verbs walk, stand, *and* sit *are common activities. The path we take is made up of dozens of ordinary choices every day. Discuss some of those everyday decisions you make, especially the ones involving other people's advice or influence. Who influences you the most in these decisions? (For example, think of social media.)*

_____

_____

_____

_____

_____

Hungering for God's Word

Second, Psalm 1:2 declares that happiness comes by developing a strong appetite for God's Word. We learn to enjoy the Bible by nurturing the disciplined habit of meditation.

Meditation involves a 24/7—"day and night"—focus on the Scripture. This means seeking to understand the Bible's meaning as well as its application to us personally. The Spirit of God makes the Word of God satisfying to the soul of man. Scripture is "sweeter than honey" (Ps. 119:103) and "more to be desired [desirable] are they than gold"; (Ps. 19:10).

Look up Joshua 1:7-8. How do these verses help us understand biblical meditation?

_____

_____

_____

_____

_____

In some contexts the word *meditate* can be translated *growl* or *groan* or *moan*. It conveys the idea of muttering. Perhaps you know someone who walks around mumbling to himself. We tend to view such behavior as socially odd. But the reality is that all of us talk to ourselves inside our heads all the time. There is a mental discussion going on continuously. Some people simply express parts of their dialogue audibly. This mental conversation is meditation. God blesses us as we mull over His words day and night.

Read Psalm 119:9–16. What does this passage teach? Commit yourself to mulling over these verses today. You could start by writing them on a 3 x 5 card or taking a screenshot so you can access this passage easily throughout the day.

_____

_____

_____

_____

The reason this way of life makes one so happy is that it fulfills the purpose for which we were created. God's first command to man was to "be fruitful" (Gen. 1:28). Psalm 1 describes the happy man as being "like a tree planted by the rivers of water, that bringeth forth his fruit in his season; his leaf also shall not wither; and whatsoever he doeth shall prosper" (Ps. 1:3).

Fruit bearing is the result of deep roots finding an abundant supply of nourishment from underground streams of water. God's Word is an all-sufficient, eternal supply of empowering grace for all of life. Even during difficult, seemingly barren times, the Word will sustain life.

A fruitful life is a blessed life. So David states that God's way to happiness is being separated from the world, saturated with the Word, and fruitful and successful in doing God's will.

It is not coincidental that Jesus begins His Sermon on the Mount with a series of Beatitudes—statements that begin with this same word, blessed. This word means to flourish. Read Matthew 5:3–12 to fill out the picture of what human flourishing looks like. Notice also that these characteristics are not what our culture typically seeks after.

The Wrong Way

Psalm 1:4–6

The ungodly are not so: but are like the chaff which the wind driveth away. Therefore the ungodly shall not stand in the judgment, nor sinners in the congregation of the righteous. For the Lord knoweth the way of the righteous: but the way of the ungodly shall perish.

David goes on in verse 4 to contrast the way of the righteous with the way of the ungodly: "the ungodly are not so." Spurgeon makes a powerful point when he notes that the Hebrew proposes a double negative: "'*Not so the ungodly, not so.*' Oh! how terrible is it to have a double negative put upon the promises! and yet this is just the condition of the ungodly."[3]

Ungodliness will never, never prosper! In the end ungodly people's lives are deemed as "chaff." In other words, they are worthless, lifeless, and useless. They will be driven away by the wind of God's judgment. They will not dwell with the people of God in the congregation of the righteous (Ps. 1:5).

At the end of the passage, the psalmist sets forth two directions—the way of the righteous and the way of the ungodly; two decisions—to meditate on God's Word or to listen to ungodly counsel; and two destinies—the righteous will enjoy God's presence forever, but the ungodly will perish.

Take some time to reflect on your life in relationship to the truth of Psalm 1. What direction are you heading? Are you developing a strong appetite for God's Word? If necessary, renew your commitment to walking in the way of God's Word.

_____

_____

_____

_____

---

[3]Spurgeon, 1:3.

Begin a biography of God by writing or typing truths that these psalms teach about Him. Later, you can organize by theme or attribute. What should you add to your biography of God from Psalm 1?

_____

_____

_____

_____

_____

Notes

03

PSALM 15
HOW TO WORSHIP GOD

The gospel turns the duty of doing and experiencing God's will into a delight.[1]

We are created for worship. The most natural thing for man to do is to devote his heart, passion, dreams, and energies to something or someone. Take away worship, and life has no meaning. Worship is intertwined with what it means to be human. If we refuse to worship God, we resort to worshiping some kind of idol (Rom. 1:21–23). Worship is not optional!

> Exalt the Lord our God, and worship at his holy hill; for the Lord our God is holy. (Psalm 99:9)

Read Romans 1:18–32 and write down the results of worshiping idols instead of God.

_____

_____

_____

---

[1]Sinclair Ferguson, *Devoted to God: Blueprints for Sanctification* (Carlisle, PA: Banner of Truth, 2016), 53.

The greatest command and the greatest calling for believers is to worship God. "O worship the Lord in the beauty of holiness: fear before him, all the earth" (Ps. 96:9). The question is: How do we worship God?

Psalm 15 was written to answer this question. The occasion of the psalm is unknown. Perhaps worshipers sang it as they journeyed to Jerusalem to worship God in the temple during the three annual Jewish festivals. Spurgeon suggests it was written after the ark was brought to Jerusalem under David's direction. In his first attempt to move the ark, David failed to follow the law's directions, and the results were devastating (2 Sam. 6:1–7). On his second attempt, David obeyed the commands of the Lord concerning the manner in which the ark was to be moved (1 Chron. 15:1–2).[2]

God does not give us the option to worship according to our own designs. There is no such thing as alternative worship. Biblical worship is prescriptive. It is to be regulated by God's Word. In Psalm 15, David asks a convicting question (v. 1) and then gives a clarifying answer (vs. 2–5) concerning how we prepare ourselves to enter into the holy presence of God to worship.

Who Can Worship God?

Psalm 15:1

Lord, who shall abide in thy tabernacle? who shall dwell in thy holy hill?

---

[2]Spurgeon, 1:176.

David is referring to both places where God's presence dwelt and where the Jewish people were to worship God—the tabernacle (a tent) and the temple (a building) on Mount Zion in Jerusalem.

Who is permitted to come and worship a holy God? This is a convicting question. If God is too pure to look upon evil (Hab. 1:13), then who is qualified to have intimate fellowship with Him? If perfect angels humbly bow before God in reverence and awe and cry, "Holy, holy, holy" (Isa. 6:3), then what should sinful humans do when seeking to come into God's presence? Is anyone worthy enough to stand before God?

The message of Scripture is that there is only one who is worthy—Jesus Christ!

> Worthy is the Lamb that was slain to receive power, and riches, and wisdom, and strength, and honour, and glory, and blessing. (Rev. 5:12)

By His sinless life and perfect obedience, Jesus entered into heaven on the merits of His own righteousness. He now intercedes on our behalf as our mediator before the Father's throne above. It is only through Him and by Him that we can have entrance into God's holy place.

> Having therefore, brethren, boldness to enter into the holiest by the blood of Jesus, by a new and living way, which he hath consecrated for us, through the veil, that is to say, his flesh. (Heb. 10:19–20)

We have access to worship God only when we humbly repent of our sins and fully depend on the blood of Christ. We cannot worship God unless we are in Christ.

 Read Hebrews 7:25–27. Meditate (i.e., start a mental conversation) on Jesus Christ's once-for-all sacrifice in

your place. Write out what that means for your worship today.

_____

_____

_____

_____

_____

What Are the Qualifications to Worship God?

David gives a clarifying answer to his rhetorical question. Through Christ we gain access to worship God, but this does not preclude the necessity of righteous living in order to worship God.

In the Old Testament there were strict regulations for the kinds of sacrifices that could be offered to God. Likewise, when you come to God, there are specific requirements for worshiping God acceptably.

We should not find this strange. When Paul gave directions concerning the Lord's Supper, he commanded believers to search their hearts: "But let a man examine himself" (1 Cor. 11:28). Therefore, in order to worship God we must search our own hearts and judge our own actions. We do not earn the right to be in God's presence by living righteously, but holiness is necessary to abide there and truly worship the Lord. Derek Kidner explains, "Indeed the question of [Psalm 15] verse 1 spoke of dwelling rather than gaining admission, for the qualities the psalm describes are those that God creates in a man, not those he finds in him."[3]

 God no longer localizes His presence, like in the Old Testament. Read John 4:21-26 and write down how Jesus' teaching relates to Psalm 15. Take note of phrases such as "in spirit," which means "from the heart," and "in truth," which means "according to Scripture."

_____

_____

_____

_____

_____

Right Conduct

Psalm 15:2

He that walketh uprightly, and worketh righteousness, and speaketh the truth in his heart.

Worship is usually associated with ritual. World religions emphasize what people must *do* in order to gain the favor of their deities. Sometimes that means offering animal sacrifices as food to their gods. Sometimes that means chanting sacred words. Sometimes that means performing painful sacraments, like ascending steps on bare knees.

Ceremony in and of itself is not evil. The Old Testament is full of it, and New Testament worship includes habitual practices as well (e.g., the public reading of Scripture; 1 Tim. 4:13). But

[3]Derek Kidner, *Psalms 1–72: An Introduction and Commentary*, ed. D. J. Wiseman (Downers Grove, IL: InterVarsity Press, 1973), 99.

David answers the question about qualifications for worship, not in terms of ceremony but of faithful living.

These three participles—*walketh*, *worketh*, and *speaketh*—refer to the actions and habits of a sound spiritual life. In order to worship God, our daily lifestyle must be blameless. We must live in conformity to the commands of God's Word. We must speak with our mouths what is consistent with our hearts. All these things are necessary for entering into spiritual fellowship with God. Hypocrisy in worship is when we say spiritual words without engaging our hearts, or when we profess to have integrity that does not match how we actually live.

Right Conversation

Psalm 15:3

He that backbiteth not with his tongue, nor doeth evil to his neighbour, nor taketh up a reproach against his neighbour.

The word *devil* means *slanderer*. Satan spoke three times that are recorded in the Bible. Each time his words were intended to destroy trust in another person (Gen. 3; Job 1–2; Matt. 4). We cannot praise God and, at the same time, curse men (James 3:9–10). We should never do wrong to another human being, especially our closest friends or relatives. We should never demean or discredit another person. Our words must build up and not tear down (Eph. 4:29).

Right Commitments

Psalm 15:4

In whose eyes a vile person is contemned; but he honoureth them that fear the Lord. He that sweareth to his own hurt, and changeth not.

True worshipers must choose to worship with those who fear the Lord. Those who are morally defiled and corrupt are to be rejected.

Furthermore, we are to keep the promises we make. Even if it is painful or leads to personal loss, we should keep the pledges we make. This includes things such as marriage, loans, and promises. These are all commitments we must keep as we seek to enter into God's worship.

Psalm 15:5

He that putteth not out his money to usury, nor taketh reward against the innocent.

Nothing reveals the nature of the heart more than our use of money. Entering into worship requires that we treat others right in our finances. The law strictly prohibited Jews from loaning their money to a fellow Israelite with interest. Bribes were also forbidden because they provoked people to violate moral principles.

When seeking to worship God, our consciences must be right in relation to our finances. Ultimately, we must not use money for selfish advantage. People are more important than money, so we should use it to help and serve others (Eph. 4:28; Acts 20:35).

Conclusion

David concludes Psalm 15 with a promise of permanence.

Psalm 15:5

He that doeth these things shall never be moved.

If we heed the spiritual conditions for worship, we will never be shaken. We will stand firm.

Dr. William Barrick offers five important applications from Psalm 15:[4]

- "Worship should not be overly casual."
- "The heart is important."
- "Relationships are important."
- "How we handle our money is important."
- "None of us can accomplish these things in our own wisdom or power."

What did you learn from Psalm 15 about worship? Which of the three areas of qualification—conduct, conversation, and commitment—is most challenging? After your discussion, turn Psalm 15 into a personal prayer.

What truths about God came to light as a result of your studying Psalm 15? Add those to your biography of God.

[4]William D. Barrick, "Psalms, Hymns, and Spiritual Songs: The Master Musician's Melodies," 2003, http://drbarrick.org/files/studynotes/Psalms/Ps_015.pdf.

Notes

04

PSALM 19
Glory to God

I take this to be the greatest poem in the Psalter and one
of the greatest lyrics in the world.[1]

I n his famous dissertation, *The End for Which God Created
the World*, Jonathan Edwards, the great American theolo-
gian, proclaimed that God's ultimate end is the manifestation
of His glory.[2] This glory is God's unique excellence—the total-
ity of His intrinsic perfections on display. We cannot pursue
life's ultimate purpose until we realize God created us to discover and declare His glory (1 Cor. 10:31).

The theme of Psalm 19 is the glory of God displayed through
the world He created (19:1–6) and the Word He spoke (19:7–
14)—or through what we call natural and special revelation.

---

[1]C. S. Lewis, *Reflection on the Psalms* (San Francisco: HarperCollins,
1958), 73.

[2]Jonathan Edwards, *Dissertation I: Concerning the End for which
God Created the World*, http://edwards.yale.edu/archive?path=aHR0c-
DovL2Vkd2FyZHMueWFsZS5lZHUvY2dpLWJpbi9uZXdwaGlsby9nZX-
RvYmplY3QucGw/Yy43OjU6Mi53amVn.

God's Glory Is Declared Through His World

Psalm 19:1

The heavens declare the glory of God; and the firmament sheweth his handywork.

David begins by asserting that all of creation displays the glory of God. The entire heavenly panorama—the sun, stars, and planets—is telling the story of His glory. The vast expanse of creation is the work of His skillful hands. All nature shouts that God is divine, all-powerful, and all-wise.

Paul affirms the truth of natural revelation in Romans 1:20. What characteristics of natural revelation does this verse teach?

_____

_____

_____

_____

_____

Psalm 19:2–3

Day unto day uttereth speech, and night unto night sheweth knowledge. There is no speech nor language, where their voice is not heard.

Every hour of every day God's message gushes forth like a mighty spring of water. Volumes are being communicated 24/7 about the knowledge of God. There is no language on earth that doesn't hear God's voice. He is not silent! If anyone claims to be an atheist, it is because he is deaf to the voice of creation.

> Nevertheless he left not himself without witness,
> in that he did good, and gave us rain from heaven,
> and fruitful seasons, filling our hearts with food
> and gladness. (Acts 14:17)

Psalm 19:4–6

Their line is gone out through all the earth, and their words to the end of the world. In them hath he set a tabernacle for the sun, which is as a bridegroom coming out of his chamber, and rejoiceth as a strong man to run a race. His going forth is from the end of the heaven, and his circuit unto the ends of it: and there is nothing hid from the heat thereof.

David uses the sun to illustrate how nature reveals God's wisdom. The psalmist describes the heavens above the earth as a huge tent with the sun lighting the space like a torch. When the sun rises in the morning, its radiant brilliance is like a bridegroom who comes out of his tent beaming with happiness. And when the sun moves in its circuit around the earth, it is like an Olympic winner who enjoys running his course.

> The glory of God is clearly seen in the sun. As it makes its daily journey across the skies, it pours out its heat on every creature, making its presence felt. So it is with God, making himself known through the sun.[3]

By pointing to the sun as God's creative handiwork, David also dismantles the idol worship of the day represented in the sun gods.

---

[3]Steven J. Lawson, *Holman Old Testament Commentary –Psalms*, ed. Max Anders (Nashville: B & H Publishing Group, 2003), 100.

What dominant ideas or cultural practices (modern idols) does the doctrine of divine creation expose and dismantle?

_____

_____

_____

_____

_____

God's Glory Is Declared Through His Word

We can know that God exists through creation, but general revelation is insufficient for knowing the fullness of God's character. It is only through Scripture that we are able to more fully comprehend the nature of God.

In Psalm 19:7–9 David gives us, as described by Spurgeon, "six descriptive titles of the word, six characteristic qualities mentioned and six divine effects declared."[4] It is as if David picks up a diamond, turns it six different ways, and expresses the brilliance of each facet.

Psalm 19:7
The law of the Lord is perfect, converting the soul:

The Hebrew word for *law* is *torah*. It refers to the first five books of the Old Testament (Genesis through Deuteronomy). However, it doesn't refer merely to laws, but rather to the doctrine or teaching of these books. The law is sufficient ("perfect") for all the needs of the spiritual life of God's children and

---

[4]Spurgeon, 1:272.

is effective to turn back and restore ("converting") us when we sin and stray from God.

Psalm 19:7

The testimony of the Lord is sure, making wise the simple.

A *testimony* is a principle found in the law that requires obedience and serves as a warning if not kept. These regulations are right and reliable. The Bible's narratives consistently show what happens when people obey and disobey God. God gave these testimonies to guide the young and naïve into all wisdom concerning righteous living.

Psalm 19:8

The statutes of the Lord are right, rejoicing the heart:

When a doctor gives you the right medicine to deal with your sickness, it makes you happy. In an even more important way, God's precepts are medicine for our souls. They are right for us and bring joy and happiness when followed.

> Thy words were found, and I did eat them; and thy word was unto me the joy and rejoicing of mine heart. (Jer. 15:16)

Psalm 19:8

The commandment of the Lord is pure, enlightening the eyes.

God's commands are pure, directing our lives morally and doctrinally into the light of God. Otherwise, we stumble along in darkness. As the psalmist prayed, "Thy word is a lamp unto my feet, and a light unto my path" (Ps. 119:105).

Read Ephesians 4:17–24. What do these verses teach about the difference between our natural darkness and our new life in Christ?

_____

_____

_____

_____

_____

Psalm 19:9
The fear of the Lord is clean, enduring for ever:

When we spend time in the Word of God, it creates within us a reverential respect for God and a hatred for sin. This attitude towards sin is not hopelessly old-fashioned but eternally relevant for all people in all times.

> Mr. Godly fear is never satisfied till every street, lane, and alley, yea, and every house and every corner of the town of Mansoul is clean rid of the Diabolonians who lurk therein.[5]

Psalm 19:9
The judgments of the Lord are true and righteous altogether.

God's declarations about what is right and wrong are reliable and trustworthy. You can build your life on all the divine standards of Scripture.

Psalm 19:10–11
More to be desired are they than gold, yea, than much fine

---

[5]Spurgeon, 1: 273, referring to John Bunyan's *The Holy War.*

gold: sweeter also than honey and the honeycomb. Moreover by them is thy servant warned: and in keeping of them there is great reward.

David ends this section by stating the immeasurable value of the Word of God. As we feed on God's truth, we discover that our souls are satisfied and delighted. It's like having the sweet taste of honey perpetually in our mouths. As we dig into God's truth, we find that what we are mining is pure gold. The Bible enriches those who engage in learning it. God's Word also protects us by admonishing us to avoid the destructive pathways of sin. Finally, God promises abundant, rewarding consequences if we strive to keep His Word by preserving, protecting, and obeying it.

Conclusion

David's conclusion to Psalm 19 links back to its introduction— God's perfections have been put on display. He concludes with His desire to conform to that glory. David turns his eyes from the *world* and the *Word* back to *himself*. Suddenly he becomes acutely aware of his own sinfulness. In light of this astonishing knowledge of God, David realizes what little knowledge he has of himself.

So the psalm concludes with a penetrating question and an earnest prayer.

Psalm 19:12
Who can understand his errors?

Can anyone really comprehend God's glorious perfections? Can anyone truly discern his own mistakes in the light of his ignorance of God's glory? The starting point of conforming to God's glory is answering David's question with humility.

He best knows himself who best knows the Word,

but even such an one will be in a maze of wonder as to what he does not know, rather than on the mount of congratulation as to what he does know.[6]

Psalm 19:12

Cleanse thou me from secret faults.

When we properly view ourselves in light of God's perfections, we are awakened to the reality that we cannot hide our secrets. God knows, God sees, God comprehends, and God judges everything about us. So our earnest prayer should be for a deep cleansing of our own internal spiritual toxins.

Psalm 19:13

Keep back thy servant also from presumptuous sins; let them not have dominion over me:

Knowing ourselves should also lead to fearing ourselves, just as Paul cried out, "O, wretched man that I am" (Rom. 7:24). We must depend on God to protect us from ourselves! Knowing our flesh is weak, even when our spirit is willing (Matt. 26:41), we should echo what Christ taught us to pray, "Lead us [me] not into temptation, but deliver us [me] from evil" (Matt. 6:13).

Presumptuous sins are rooted in pride. The viewpoint of our flesh is "I can handle this." Self-reliance causes many failures. Therefore our greatest protection from sin is humility before God.

Psalm 19:14

Let the words of my mouth, and the meditation of my heart, be acceptable in thy sight, O Lord, my strength, and my redeemer.

---

[6]Spurgeon, 1:274.

David's earnest prayer is for internal spiritual transparency before God. Hypocrisy is the religious man's favorite sin. It is disingenuous to live one way before man and another way before God. David was passionate about living sincerely before God. He prayed that his verbal communications and internal meditations would be pleasing in God's sight!

In the end this would not be possible without God being our strength (rock), our deliverer and restorer (Redeemer).

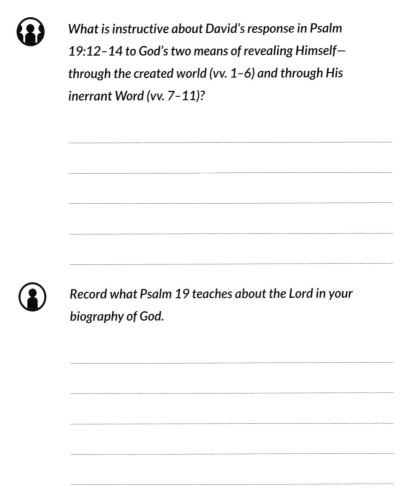

What is instructive about David's response in Psalm 19:12–14 to God's two means of revealing Himself— through the created world (vv. 1–6) and through His inerrant Word (vv. 7–11)?

Record what Psalm 19 teaches about the Lord in your biography of God.

Apply Psalm 19 to yourself in prayer. Here is an example:

Dear God, You are full of glory. You are perfect in all Your ways. What You have made testifies to Your power, Your wisdom, and Your deity. Every morning I awake and see Your glory in all You have made. The sun speaks of Your light, Your presence, and the warmth of Your love. You are God! Thank You for Your Word. Thank You for revealing Yourself to me. Open my eyes to understand Your law. Help me to walk in Your ways. Cleanse me from my secret sins. Guard me from my own selfish desires and protect me from self-reliance and pride. Help me to live transparently before You in how I think and speak. You, O God, are my rock and my Redeemer!

Notes

05

PSALM 23
Jesus is My Shepherd

The personal way in which the psalmist speaks of God, the imagery of God's soothing guidance, and the ensuing confidence in God have all been factors in making this one of the most charming and beloved of the Psalms.[1]

Everyone needs a shepherd. We can't go through life without one. We need someone who can guide our steps, guard us from danger, and lead us to places of nourishment and satisfaction. We need a shepherd.

If anyone understood shepherding, it was David. From his earliest years he tended his father's flock (1 Sam. 16:11). Later God chose him to leave the sheepfolds to become king and shepherd of Israel (1 Chron. 11:2; Ps. 78:70). Throughout his own spiritual experience David testified that the Lord was his Shepherd. It should not surprise us that God chose David to author Psalm 23.

This psalm begins with a confident declaration: "The Lord is my shepherd." The meaning of the name *Lord* is very important. This is God's personal name. The Hebrew word is *YHWH*.

---

[1]Willem A. VanGemeren, *The Expositor's Bible Commentary: Psalms, Proverbs, Ecclesiastes, Song of Songs*, ed. Frank E. Gaebelein (Grand Rapids: Zondervan, 1991), 5:214.

It is often translated *Jehovah* or *Yahweh* and occurs over 6,800 times in the Old Testament. The Lord defined the meaning of His name to Moses by declaring, "I AM THAT I AM" (Ex. 3:14). In other words, He is the self-existing God. His existence depends on no one else. Rather everyone else depends on Him for their existence. Remarkably, in John 8:58, Jesus used this same sacred name to refer to Himself when He said, "Before Abraham was, I am." Jesus affirmed that He is the Lord of the Old Testament. He also identifies Himself as the Good Shepherd (John 10:11). So it is appropriate for Christians to say, "Jesus is my Shepherd."

What does it mean for Jesus Christ to be our Shepherd? Psalm 23 describes seven ways.

He Owns Me

Psalm 23:1

The Lord is my shepherd;

To say "The Lord is my shepherd" does not mean that I own Him but that He owns me. The shepherd owns the sheep; they are his property. They are not wild animals like wolves. He purchases them at a price and cares for them with love.

What does it mean for Jesus to *own* us? First, as our Good Shepherd, Jesus paid the price of His own life for His sheep. He said, "I am the good shepherd: the good shepherd giveth his life for the sheep" (John 10:11). He laid down His life in death on a cross to purchase us from sin. This means we belong to Him: "Know ye not that . . . ye are not your own? For ye are bought with a price" (1 Cor. 6:19–20).

Second, as our Good Shepherd, Christ has taken responsibility to care for us forever. Jacob testified to God's faithful ministry as his Shepherd: "God, before whom my fathers Abraham and

Isaac did walk, the God which fed me all my life long unto this day" (Gen. 48:15).

We can be just as confident because Christ explained, "My sheep hear my voice, and I know them, and they follow me: and I give unto them eternal life; and they shall never perish, neither shall any man pluck them out of my hand" (John 10:27–28). Jesus is our Shepherd right now and for eternity!

 Write down some ways in which the Lord has shepherded you to this point in your life. Then offer a prayer of thanksgiving to Him with these specific blessings in mind.

_____

_____

_____

_____

_____

He Provides for Me

Psalm 23:1

I shall not want.

This statement does not mean God gives us everything we want. The term *want* is a way of describing need. David affirms that we will never lack what we need. The Lord will always provide. Paul reaffirms this truth in the New Testament: "But my God shall supply all your need according to his riches in glory by Christ Jesus" (Phil. 4:19).

Jesus Christ taught that when we wonder whether or not God will meet our physical needs, we should ask ourselves a few questions from Matthew 6:25–30. Does God not feed the ravens? Does He not cause the lilies to grow? How, then, can He leave his children to hunger?

What about our spiritual needs? Does our Shepherd provide for them too? Consider how Christ counseled Paul in 2 Corinthians 12:9: "My grace is sufficient for thee: for my strength is made perfect in weakness."

 Read Paul's response to Christ's counsel in 2 Corinthians 12:10. What does this verse teach us about responding when the Lord provides for our needs in a way that is different from what we expected or desired?

_____

_____

_____

_____

_____

You may wonder, how can I be absolutely confident that God will faithfully supply all my needs? Because He has already provided your greatest need—His Son as your Savior! There is hardly a more uplifting verse in all of Scripture than Romans 8:32: "He that spared not his own Son, but delivered him up for us all, how shall he not with him also freely give us all things?"

He Gives Me True Peace and Satisfaction

Psalm 23:2
He maketh me to lie down in green pastures:

Sheep are fearful, nervous, and insecure animals, always concerned about being fed and protected. The primary role of any shepherd is to take his sheep to places where they can be nourished and satisfied. He must also provide security from dangers and threats so that his sheep can lie down and be at rest.

The Lord promised to be this kind of Shepherd.

> I will feed them in a good pasture, and upon the high mountains of Israel shall their fold be: there shall they lie in a good fold, and in a fat pasture shall they feed upon the mountains of Israel. I will feed my flock, and I will cause them to lie down, saith the Lord God. (Ezek. 34:14–15)

Unlike Israel's spiritual leaders, the Lord insures that His people experience true shalom, a peace and wholeness that this world cannot provide. Jesus assures His disciples, "Peace I leave with you, my peace I give unto you: not as the world giveth, give I unto you" (John 14:27).

Psalm 23:2

He leadeth me beside the still waters.

The word *lead* means to guide to a watering place and cause to rest there. The shepherd leads his sheep to waters of rest. Sheep will not drink water out of a rapidly flowing river. Often the shepherd would take stones and dam up the running waters in order to create an oasis of calm water for his sheep to drink. The shepherd provided all the essentials: food, water, and rest.

Christ our Shepherd leads us, which means we have to follow Him. Following the shepherd requires great trust. It starts with knowing the shepherd's voice and obeying his command. Jesus taught that following is what true disciples do. "My sheep hear my voice, and I know them, and they follow me" (John 10:27).

He Restores Me

Psalm 23:3

He restoreth my soul:

Sheep by nature struggle. They are easily hurt, bruised, and cut. Perhaps you can relate to this. Therefore shepherds have to bind up the broken. This is what Christ does for His people. God promised in Ezekiel 34:16: "I will seek that which was lost, and bring again that which was driven away, and will bind up that which was broken, and will strengthen that which was sick."

Sheep also stray away from their shepherd. They are prone to wander. Jesus uses an illustration of a shepherd with a hundred sheep and one who strays away. What does the shepherd do? He searches for the one who is lost until he finds it and brings it back to the fold (Luke 15:3–7).

> For ye were as sheep going astray; but are now returned unto the Shepherd and Bishop of your souls (1 Peter 2:25).

The Lord continually restores the spiritual life of his people. He "revive[s] us again" (Ps. 85:6). He brings us back to Himself by renewing our desires, our passions, our appetites, and our emotions for God. He renews us inside by His power through His Word. As David states in a psalm we considered previously: "The law of the Lord is perfect, converting the soul" (Ps. 19:7). God's Word avails because He is the Good Shepherd.

> When the soul grows sorrowful he revives it; when it is sinful he sanctifies it; when it is weak he strengthens it.[2]

---

[2]Spurgeon, 1:355.

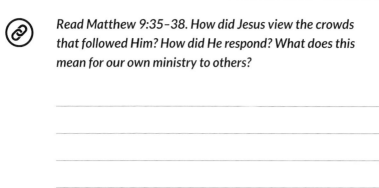

Read Matthew 9:35–38. How did Jesus view the crowds that followed Him? How did He respond? What does this mean for our own ministry to others?

_____

_____

_____

_____

_____

He Guides Me

Psalm 23:3

He leadeth me in the paths of righteousness for his name's sake.

The shepherd leads his sheep throughout the hills of Judea to fields of green grass. These hills are lined with thousands of well-worn paths. Some paths lead to food, others to cliffs and crevices where sheep could fall to their deaths. The wilderness is a place of a thousand dangers. Only the shepherd knows the right path for his sheep to take. Only the shepherd can keep his sheep from going the wrong way and getting lost or hurt.

Jesus, the Good Shepherd, is our guide. We have to acknowledge that without His direction we go astray. But by following His leadership, we honor His name.

Write out Psalm 25:4–5 and then pray for God to lead you in your current circumstances.

_____

_____

He Protects Me

Psalm 23:4

Yea, though I walk through the valley of the shadow of death, I will fear no evil: for thou art with me; Thy rod and thy staff they comfort me.

Israel is the land of hills and valleys. When shepherds lead their sheep to green pastures, they often have to pass through valleys. These valleys, called *wadis*, are dangerous places. They are normally dry river beds that contain water only during times of heavy rain. When rain comes and water flows through the wadis, they become extremely dangerous. Many unsuspecting hikers have been washed away to their deaths in them.

Valleys also become dark places when the sun is obstructed by steep cliffs. The Hebrew for the *shadow of the valley* means *a place of deep darkness* or *the place of a death shadow*. Within these valleys wild animals lurk. David fought off a lion and a bear while protecting his own flock (1 Sam. 17:37).

However, all fear is alleviated by the presence of the shepherd. As one author puts it, "We are never so conscious of the presence of God as when we pass through life's valleys."[3]

> When thou passest through the waters, I will be
> with thee; and through the rivers, they shall not

---

[3]James Montgomery Boice, *Psalms* (Grand Rapids: Baker Books, 1994), 1:211.

overflow thee: when thou walkest through the fire, thou shalt not be burned; neither shall the flame kindle upon thee. For I am the Lord thy God, the Holy One of Israel, thy Savior. (Isa. 43:2–3)

The symbols of the shepherd's office were a rod and a staff. Steve Lawson says:

> The shepherd's rod was usually an oak club about two feet long. It was used to defend the flock against wild animals . . . as well as for counting, guiding, and protecting his sheep. And the shepherd's staff was his crook. Bent or hooked at one end, it was used to pry sheep loose from thickets, to push branches aside, to pull fallen sheep out of holes, to lead them along narrow paths, and to drive off snakes. Such tools were sources of comfort for fearful sheep.[4]

He Prospers Me

Psalm 23:5
Thou preparest a table before me in the presence of mine enemies: thou anointest my head with oil; my cup runneth over.

David encountered enemies many times during his life. At the same time they were seeking to destroy him, God was prospering him.

The Hebrew word translated *table* denotes a skin or a leather mat spread out on the ground like a picnic blanket. A good shepherd always brings his flock to places where they can spread out, eat, and then lie down and rest. The word translated *anoint* often describes an animal that is fat or well-fed. A

---

[4]Lawson, 127.

fat animal was considered healthy. We often use the word *fullness*. David means that ever since the prophet Samuel anointed him, God had been pouring out rich and abundant blessings. His cup was constantly running over. He was wealthy and prosperous because of God's riches towards Him.

We may not be materially wealthy, but we are incalculably rich in Christ. As Paul exclaims, "[God] hath blessed us with all spiritual blessings in heavenly places in Christ . . . according to the riches of his grace" (Eph. 1:3, 7).

Read Paul's doxology in Ephesians 1:3–14 and list the rich spiritual blessings that are yours in Christ.

_____

_____

_____

_____

_____

Conclusion

Psalm 23:6

Surely goodness and mercy shall follow me all the days of my life: and I will dwell in the house of the Lord forever.

David concludes this Shepherd's Psalm with a testimony of his firm confidence in the Good Shepherd. *Surely* could be translated *only*. It is a statement of assurance. David was able to look back on his life and see nothing but God's goodness and mercy following him everywhere he went. Knowing the unchanging nature of God, David foresaw nothing but God's goodness and mercy following him in the future.

Spurgeon helpfully remarks,

> These twin guardian angels will always be with me at my back and my beck. Just as when great princes go abroad they must not go unattended, so it is with the believer. Goodness and mercy follow him always—all the days of his life—the black days as well as the bright days, the days of fasting as well as the days of feasting, the dreary days of winter as well as the bright days of summer. Goodness supplies our needs, and mercy blots out our sins.[5]

Because of his confidence in God's goodness and mercy, David made it his continual practice to return back to the Shepherd's house for spiritual renewal. The word *dwell* could be translated *return*. This is the same word translated *restore* in verse three. Returning time and again to the Lord and the fellowship of His saints is the path of spiritual renewal for God's children. *Forever* means *the length of days, all of one's life*, both now and for eternity.

What about God's character and ministry to sheep like us should you add to your biography of God?

_____

_____

_____

_____

_____

---

[5]Spurgeon, 1:356.

Notes

06

PSALM 51
Have Mercy on Me

> If the universe weren't ruled by a God of forgiveness,
> there would be no Psalm 51. It would be an act of self-
> destructive irrationality to stand before the One who
> controls it all and admit that you've willingly rebelled
> against his commands, but that's exactly what David does.[1]

Sin is common to mankind. There is a Creator God, and we break His laws. How do we respond to God when we sin personally? The Bible directs us to confess and forsake our sins (Prov. 28:13). Psalm 51 is one of seven penitential psalms, a type of lament (Pss. 6, 32, 38, 51, 102, 130, 143). It provides the clearest, most thorough description of confession in the Bible.

The title of this psalm clarifies both its author and setting: "To the chief Musician, A Psalm of David, when Nathan the prophet came unto him, after he had gone in to Bathsheba." The setting is found in 2 Samuel 11–12 when David committed his infamous sin of adultery with Bathsheba, the wife of one of David's mighty men, Uriah the Hittite (2 Sam. 23:39). Nathan, God's prophet, confronted David one year after the king had sinned. Psalm 51 is David's humble confession to God concerning his immoral affair with Bathsheba, which led to his murder of Uriah.

---

[1]Paul David Tripp, *Whiter Than Snow: Meditations on Sin and Mercy* (Wheaton: Crossway Books, 2008), 135.

David's Cry

Psalm 51:1–3

Have mercy upon me, O God, according to thy lovingkindness: according unto the multitude of thy tender mercies blot out my transgressions. Wash me throughly from mine iniquity, and cleanse me from my sin. For I acknowledge my transgressions: and my sin is ever before me.

From the depths of his heart, David cried to God for mercy. He pled with God to show him His undeserved grace. David knew what he deserved. What he had done was heinous in God's sight. But in spite of his personal failure, David still pursued God. Why? Because he intimately knew God. He had to be reconciled.

David Knew What God Was Like

Though David had sinned, he believed that God was committed to loving him. God's lovingkindness is a central quality of His nature. The Hebrew word *chesed* means a loyal, steadfast love based on a covenant relationship. *Tender mercies* means that God is full of a deep-seated compassion and love. David knew that God's heart was full of love for the wayward king.

David Knew What He Had Done

David uses three words to describe his sinful actions.

1. *Transgression* means *to cross the line*. It conveys the idea of rebelling against divine authority and breaking the law.
2. *Iniquity* means *to go astray*. It pictures leaving the righteous path to go in a crooked direction.
3. *Sin* means *to fall short or miss the mark*. Sinners come up short of God's standard.

When David sinned with Bathsheba, he broke the moral law of God, he perverted the intention of marriage between one man and one woman, and he fell abysmally short of living up to God's standard.

David Knew What God Could Do

David understood that God could deal with his sins thoroughly and completely.

1. **He would** *blot them out* like erasing or removing numbers from an accounting book.
2. **He would** *wash them away* like an ancient laundryman who soaked, soaped, beat, wrung out, and rinsed clothing to get it clean.
3. **He would** *cleanse them* like the process of purification in order to approach the altar or to participate in worship at the tabernacle.[2]

David knew God's character, his sinfulness, and God's redemptive ways. Discuss how these three truths are critical to dealing with our sins.

_____

_____

_____

_____

_____

[2]Paraphrase of William D. Barrick, "Psalms, Hymns, and Spiritual Songs: The Master Musician's Melodies," 2005, https://drbarrick.org/files/studynotes/Psalms/Ps_051.pdf.

David's Confession

Confession means *to say the same thing.* To confess our sins is to view them from God's perspective and agree with what He says about them. What did David confess?

David Confessed the Reality of His Sin Against God

Psalm 51:4

Against thee, thee only, have I sinned, and done this evil in thy sight: that thou mightest be justified when thou speakest, and be clear when thou judgest.

David could not escape the reality that his sin was primarily against God. He was haunted by the thought that his actions revealed that he loved himself more than he loved God. David had wronged Uriah and Bathsheba horribly, but that harm paled in comparison to his sin against God. Puritan Stephen Charnock wrote:

> All sin is founded in secret atheism. . . . All the wicked inclinations in the heart . . . are sparks from this latent fire; the language of everyone of these is, I would be Lord to myself, and would not have God superior to me. . . . A man in every sin aims to set up his own will as his rule, and his own glory as the end of his actions against the will and glory of God.[3]

David did not justify his actions by blaming others or making excuses. He simply admitted his wrong and willingly accepted God's just judgment.

---

[3]Stephen Charnock, *The Existence and Attributes of God* (Grand Rapids: Baker Books, 1996), 93–94.

Read Romans 3:1–4. This passage is near the end of a section in which Paul is explaining the sinfulness of all people. In other words, the conclusion David reached about his sin is the standpoint every sinner must take in coming to God for salvation. Is this how you typically view your sins?

_____

_____

_____

_____

_____

David Confessed the Root of His Sin

Psalm 51:5–6

Behold, I was shapen in iniquity; and in sin did my mother conceive me. Behold, thou desirest truth in the inward parts: and in the hidden part thou shalt make me to know wisdom.

The root cause of David's sin was his own nature, which he received at conception. David was a sinner long before he ever sinned. This human trait is known as *original sin*. As one author notes, "We have inherited from our first father not just a debt, but also a compulsion, a compulsion to reenact his alienation of himself from God."[4]

David laid bare his soul before God and man. He had been covering his sin and living a lie for over a year. Finally he did the wisest and only righteous thing he could do. He was truthful with himself and God and turned away from his evil.

---

[4]Alan Jacobs, *Original Sin: A Cultural History* (New York: HarperOne, 2008), 32.

The fear of the Lord is to hate evil: pride, and ar-
rogancy, and the evil way, and the froward mouth,
do I hate. (Prov. 8:13)

David's Cleansing

David then asks for a thorough personal cleansing. He wants
to be fully right and totally restored to God. This process of
cleansing includes removal, renewal, and restoration.

A Removal of Sin

Psalm 51:7
Purge me with hyssop, and I shall be clean.

David essentially asks for the same thing as he did in verses
one through three, except they are in reverse order: *cleanse,
wash, blot.* He wanted to be completely cleansed from sin.
Hyssop was a small tree branch used for cleansing ceremonies
for lepers (Lev. 14:4–6) or for those who touched dead things
(Num. 19:18). The priests dipped hyssop in blood or water
and sprinkled it on the sinner. Hyssop also was used to smear
blood on Israel's doorposts during the Passover (Ex. 12:22).

Psalm 51:7–9
*Wash me, and I shall be whiter than snow. Make me to hear
joy and gladness; that the bones which thou hast broken may
rejoice. Hide thy face from my sins, and blot out all mine iniquities.*

Under the law there was no explicit provision for the cleansing
of an adulterer. David had to look beyond the law to the heart
of God to find hope. He trusted God alone to make him so
clean that he would be "whiter than snow." David wanted God
to look at his sins no longer but totally remove them from His
record.

Isaiah had the same confidence in God's power to cleanse: "Come now, and let us reason together, saith the Lord: though your sins be as scarlet, they shall be as white as snow" (Isa. 1:18). God can make us whiter than snow through the blood of Jesus (Rev. 7:14).

Jesus said something similar to the woman caught in the act of adultery: "Neither do I condemn thee: go, and sin no more" (John 8:11). What does this passage in John teach us about God's response to great sins? What does this have to do with Isaiah 1:18 and Revelation 7:14?

A Renewal of Spirit

Psalm 51:10

Create in me a clean heart, O God; and renew a right spirit within me.

David uses the language of creation (Gen. 1:1) to describe the change he desired in his heart. He wanted his spirit to be fixed or repaired so that it would be steadfast and faithful to God. He loathed the idea of falling back into impurity.

Psalm 51:11

Cast me not away from thy presence; and take not thy holy spirit from me.

David knew and had experienced God's power in his life. He also had observed how the Spirit departed from Saul because of his rebellion and disobedience to God. David did not want to be cast aside from God's service (1 Cor. 9:27).

A Restoration of Salvation Joy

Psalm 51:12
Restore unto me the joy of thy salvation; and uphold me with thy free spirit.

David's reference to the departure of the Holy Spirit does not mean he was afraid he was not saved after all. He wanted to return to the sincere joy and happiness he had experienced because of his salvation. He was asking God to eagerly support him with His spiritual power and presence.

David's Commitment

After crying out to God in humble confession of his sin and petition for cleansing, David made commitments to God. If God would forgive him, David would gladly participate in His service by instructing others, worshiping God publicly, and demonstrating true humility.

He Would Teach Sinners the Way of Salvation

Psalm 51:13
Then will I teach transgressors thy ways; and sinners shall be converted unto thee.

David could powerfully teach sinners the way of salvation because of the testimony of his own experience of God's grace and mercy.

He Would Sing Praises to God

Psalm 51:14–15

Deliver me from bloodguiltiness, O God, thou God of my salvation: and my tongue shall sing aloud of thy righteousness. O Lord, open thou my lips; and my mouth shall shew forth thy praise.

God created us to praise Him. David lost his spirit of praise because he had covered his sin. He lived with the burden and guilt of stealing the wife of Uriah and then shedding his innocent blood. However, if God would free him from that guilt, David would be free to sing and praise God again.

He Would Offer Acceptable Sacrifices to God

Psalm 51:16–17

For thou desirest not sacrifice; else would I give it: thou delightest not in burnt offering. The sacrifices of God are a broken spirit: a broken and a contrite heart, O God, thou wilt not despise.

The sacrifices that the Israelites offered to God in the temple were supposed to reflect the inner heart of the worshiper. God had no desire to receive a broken animal sacrifice unless the one giving the offering did so with a broken, contrite heart. "Man looketh on the outward appearance, but the Lord looketh on the heart" (1 Sam. 16:7).

 Read Isaiah 57:15 and 66:1–2. What do these verses teach about the Lord God and His relationship to mankind?

_____

_____

_____

David's Conclusion

Psalm 51:18–19

Do good in thy good pleasure unto Zion: build thou the walls of Jerusalem. Then shalt thou be pleased with the sacrifices of righteousness, with burnt offering and whole burnt offering: then shall they offer bullocks upon thine altar.

God established the sacrificial offering system as the means by which His people individually and collectively could worship and maintain a right relationship with Him. When God accepted these sacrifices He was honored and His blessings flowed. To humble, forgiven people God will grant peace and prosperity, as well as protection to the city of Jerusalem.

Our flesh tempts us to justify our wrong actions and to cover our sin. But those who do so never prosper (Prov. 28:13). Following the inspired example David records in Psalm 51 is the only way to deal with our sin and experience true peace.

What did you learn from Psalm 51 about encountering the living God? Write that down in your biography of God. Take some time to review the biography you have compiled from Psalms so far.

What did you learn about confession of sin from studying this psalm? Did the Lord expose any needs in your own soul? Follow David's example and lay bare your soul before Him.

_____

_____

_____

_____

_____

Notes

07

PSALM 90
Living with an Eternal Perspective

All that is temporal is ultimately trivial. What is truly important in the present is that which will be important ten thousand years from today.[1]

According to its title, "A Prayer of Moses the man of God," Psalm 90 was authored by Moses. Since he lived around 1400 BC, this means Psalm 90 is the oldest of the psalms and Moses is the first composer of sacred hymnody.

 The title refers to Moses as "the man of God." Look up the other six times Scripture uses this designation: Deuteronomy 33:1; Joshua 14:6; 1 Chronicles 23:14; 2 Chronicles 30:16; Ezra 3:2. Do you see any patterns or similar emphases?

---

[1]Steven J. Lawson, *Holman Old Testament Commentary—Psalms 76–150*, ed. Max Anders (Nashville: Broadman & Holman Publishers, 2006), 81.

Moses was called "the man of God" because he mediated between God and the children of Israel. He served by interceding for the children of Israel in prayer and invoking God's blessing upon them. A true man of God is a man of prayer. Therefore, Psalm 90 is called "A Prayer of Moses the man of God."

In this case Moses was praying for the children of Israel to learn an important life lesson. The lesson was something he had learned through his experience of wandering in the wilderness with them. What should have been a relatively short journey from Egypt to Israel turned out to be a forty-year excursion of defeat, discouragement, and death. The lesson that Moses learned during this time was to live purposefully in light of eternity.

The events of Numbers 20 may be the historical background for Psalm 90. Moses' sister Miriam died (Num. 20:1), Moses sinned against God by striking the rock (20:2–13), and Moses' brother Aaron died (20:22–29). These successive events reinforce this truth: in light of the brevity of our lives, we must learn to live wisely, dependent upon God.

The reality of eternity serves as a vital motivation for those who make a significant impact on the world for Christ. It is said that Jonathan Edwards memorably prayed, "Lord, stamp eternity on my eyeballs."

God Is Eternal

Psalm 90:1–2

Lord, thou hast been our dwelling place in all generations. Before the mountains were brought forth, or ever thou hadst formed the earth and the world, even from everlasting to everlasting, thou art God.

The psalm begins with the unfathomable truth that God existed in eternity past. God created all that exists in the world today. God will continue to exist long after this world is gone. Only God is eternally constant.

By way of contrast, Moses and the children of Israel lived in tents for forty years while journeying through the wilderness as nomads. They had two constant experiences during this time—packing up tents and attending funerals. They lived in a permanent state of flux. The only thing that was consistent for the homeless children of God was the presence of the Lord dwelling among them.

No matter where we live in this ever-changing world, our souls will feel at rest only when the eternal God is with us. The everlasting Lord is our dwelling place. He is the one who makes us feel at home!

1 John 5:20 says, "And we know that the Son of God is come, and hath given us an understanding, that we may know him that is true, and we are in him that is true, even in his Son Jesus Christ. This is the true God, and eternal life." Only in our union with Jesus Christ by faith can we experience eternal life. Otherwise our lives have only temporal purpose and pleasure.

Man Is Temporal

Against the backdrop of God's eternality, Moses starkly portrays the frailty and finitude of human existence. We are formations of dust that live for a brief time and are subject to the righteous wrath of God.

Man's Origin Is Humble

Psalm 90:3

Thou turnest man to destruction; and sayest, Return, ye children of men.

Our original composition is dust (Gen. 2:7). Our final destination is back to the dust. We never really get above the dirt beneath our feet. It is appropriately humbling to remember that our final destiny in this life is death and that our bodies will decay. Death is the great equalizer. Rich and poor, famous and obscure, intellectual and illiterate, humanitarian and criminal—all of us end up decomposing six feet under.

> In the sweat of thy face shalt thou eat bread, till thou return unto the ground; for out of it wast thou taken: for dust thou art, and unto dust shalt thou return. (Gen. 3:19)

Man's Lifespan Is Brief

Psalm 90:4

For a thousand years in thy sight are but as yesterday when it is past, and as a watch in the night.

Moses contrasts God's perspective on time with a human point of view. Everything in God's eyes is either smaller in size or shorter in time. For example, God sees the population of the nations "as a drop of a bucket":

> Behold, the nations are as a drop of a bucket, and are counted as the small dust of the balance. (Isa. 40:15)

Similarly, in God's eyes one thousand years are like a day that has already passed by or like a four-hour watch in the night (Ps. 90:4). A long, full life seems like an eternity when we are young. But time marches on at warp speed.

Man's Death Is Swift

Psalm 90:5–6

Thou carriest them away as with a flood; they are as a sleep: In the morning they are like grass which groweth up. In the morning it flourisheth, and groweth up; in the evening it is cut down, and withereth.

The sobering realities of our humble origins and brief life-span point toward a third: life ends suddenly. With three natural images Moses depicts how quickly death descends on us: floods, dreams, and grass.

First, death is like a sudden flood. In the land of Israel, one of the most dangerous threats to human life is a flash flood in a wadi.

Moses also says that life is like a dream. While we are sleeping, our dreams seem so real. We find ourselves deeply engaged in fantasy until we suddenly awaken to realize the dream has vanished.

During the winter rains in Israel, the grass quickly pops up on the hills in the Judean wilderness only to wither away in the scorching heat of the spring. We are not like trees that stand tall, pointing toward the skies. We are like the grass that bends low and hovers slightly above the dirt.

 Read Ecclesiastes 11:9–12:14 together. Discuss the divine wisdom given in the conclusion to this book, particularly as it applies to youth.

_____

_____

_____

_____

_____

God's Judgment Is Just

Psalm 90:7–9

For we are consumed by thine anger, and by thy wrath are we troubled. Thou hast set our iniquities before thee, our secret sins in the light of thy countenance. For all our days are passed away in thy wrath: we spend our years as a tale that is told.

The Jewish people received a firsthand experience of God's just judgment in the wilderness. An entire generation was buried in the desert sand because of its sin. The Lord would not allow the Israelites to forget their idolatry, rebellion, immorality, and murmuring. Their circumstances were a daily reminder of God's judgment for what they had done.

Moses says that the people lived with the knowledge that they were under a death sentence. At the end of their lives, all they could do was sigh with a sense of sadness and emptiness as they drew their last breath.

We may be tempted to protest that the brevity of life is unfair. Why do we have to die so soon, some even sooner than others? Read Romans 5:12. What does it teach about the just judgment of God upon all people, not just Israel?

_____

_____

_____

_____

_____

Psalm 90:10–12

The days of our years are threescore years and ten; and if by reason of strength they be fourscore years, yet is their strength labour and sorrow; for it is soon cut off, and we fly away. Who knoweth the power of thine anger? even according to thy fear, so is thy wrath. So teach us to number our days, that we may apply our hearts unto wisdom.

Our lives are short. We live to be seventy; some make it to eighty. We have enough strength to work for a few years, and then we become old and fly away in death. We are all terminal because of God's righteous curse on our sin, yet most people do not understand God's anger against sin.

These verses should cause us to realize that time is not a commodity to waste. We have only so much of it. Once time is gone, we cannot get it back. We must take an accounting of the number of days we have to live so that we do not waste an hour but invest our lives in what is eternal.

 Take an accounting of how you have used the past seventy-two hours. Could you be more purposeful in investing your life in what is eternal? How?

_____

_____

_____

_____

_____

Prayer Is Essential

In verse 3 of Psalm 90, God calls man to return to Him. In verse 13 the psalmist calls on God to return to man. Our necessary response to the brevity of life is to cry out to God in prayer. This is what Moses does in Psalm 90:13–17.

Pray for Mercy

Psalm 90:13–14

Return, O Lord, how long? and let it repent thee concerning thy servants. O satisfy us early with thy mercy; that we may rejoice and be glad all our days.

God's people had suffered under God's chastening hand for a long time. Moses wondered aloud how long it would continue. God had made a covenant with His people through Abraham and David—a covenant backed by God's own faithfulness and love. Moses prayed for God to return back to His people and show His loyal love based on His covenant commitment.

Pray for Joy

Psalm 90:15

Make us glad according to the days wherein thou hast afflicted us, and the years wherein we have seen evil.

God's people had suffered because of their sin. Now they longed for a restoration of true joy. True forgiveness will bring true fellowship with God and a reversal from sadness to gladness among His people.

Psalm 126 expresses a similar experience. The background of this psalm is that Israel had gone into captivity because of sin. They had wept much. Their prayer was for a turning—for God to bring them back to their land and restore their lost joy.

> Turn again our captivity, O Lord, as the streams in the south. They that sow in tears shall reap in joy. He that goeth forth and weepeth, bearing precious seed, shall doubtless come again with rejoicing, bringing his sheaves with him. (Ps. 126:4–6)

Pray for Blessing

Psalm 90:16–17

Let thy work appear unto thy servants, and thy glory unto their children. And let the beauty of the Lord our God be upon us: and establish thou the work of our hands upon us; yea, the work of our hands establish thou it.

Israel's wilderness wanderings were a forty-year exercise in circular futility. God's people simply survived. However, they learned one unforgettable lesson. Their experience in the desert created a passionate desire to get into the promised land of God's blessing. At the end of Psalm 90, Moses prays for God to do His work and manifest His glory in the midst of His people.

Moses finishes this psalm with a prayer for God's favor (beauty) to be on His people and for their work to prosper in God's hand. His desire is for their work to be solidified and enduring as they depend on God.

Our time on earth is short in light of eternity. We must seek God in prayer for His mercy, His joy, and ultimately, His blessing upon all that we do in this life.

Prayer: Dear Heavenly Father, we find no rest until we rest in You. Our sins are always before us. Have mercy upon us and forgive us. You are eternal and unchanging. Our lives are brief, and we are consumed by death. Help us to have the wisdom to use our days to fulfill your work in this world. Fill us with the joy and blessing of Your presence. Make the work that we do solid. Prosper us as we serve You. Till the end of our lives, may we honor and glorify Your name.

 Add to your biography of God based on Psalm 90.

Notes

08

PSALM 100
Jubilate

> Approaching God is a high privilege for all believers.
> Such an audience before heaven's King should be
> carried out with the reverence of one coming before
> the monarch of the universe. . . . All believers must
> come properly before God's throne in worship. Such
> a privileged audience before the sovereign King
> requires gladness of heart, joyful singing, expressions of
> thanksgiving, and songs of praise.[1]

The title of Psalm 100, "A Psalm of praise," is unique. No other psalm begins this way. Therefore, Psalm 100 reveals a special emphasis for God's people.

Some writers have suggested that this psalm was sung at the time when thank offerings were being made during temple worship. These thank offerings were expressions of gratitude to God for His special deliverance and protection. Thank offerings accompanied peace offering sacrifices (Lev. 7:11–12) that were to be eaten with the priests as fellowship meals in the temple (Lev. 3:3–5).

> Offer unto God thanksgiving; and pay thy vows
> unto the most High: And call upon me in the day
> of trouble: I will deliver thee, and thou shalt glorify
> me. (Ps. 50:14–15)

Others have suggested that this psalm was sung by pilgrims in a procession as they were going to the temple in Jerusalem

---

[1]Lawson, *Holman Old Testament Commentary–Psalms 76–150*, 135.

during religious festivals. This procession continues today when young Jewish men in Jerusalem coming from a yeshiva sing in a procession as they make their way to the Kotel (Western Wall) for Shabbat (Sabbath) prayers.

In either case, whether it's during an offering or a procession, Psalm 100 serves to instruct us in the art and the heart of worship. A. W. Tozer described worship as "the missing jewel in the church." He went on to say, "God wants worshipers before workers; indeed, the only acceptable workers are those who have learned the art of worship."[2]

The focus of our worship according to Psalm 100 is the Lord Himself. We are to come into His presence for His sake alone. Worship is not about us. Worship is not a means to an end. It is an end in itself. It's all about God! We will never get "church" right if we don't get worship right. The church gets off track when worship is no longer the engine that drives it.

So how do we appropriately worship God? The author gives seven divine imperatives that direct our approach to God in worship.

Shout

Psalm 100:1

Make a joyful noise unto the Lord, all ye lands.

Dan Forrest, acclaimed composer of choral works, masterfully composed the text of Psalm 100 into seven different languages. The title of his work, *Jubilate Deo*, comes from the opening

---

[2]A. W. Tozer, *That Incredible Christian: How Heaven's Children Live on Earth*, comp. Anita M. Bailey (Camp Hill, PA: WingSpread Publishers, 2008), 37.

phrase of the psalm in Latin—"O be joyful in the Lord." The Latin word *jubilate* means to shout for joy! What kind of shout is this? It is the fanfare and celebration that takes place in the presence of the king.

> And Samuel said to all the people, See ye him whom the Lord hath chosen, that there is none like him among all the people? And all the people shouted, and said, God save the king. (1 Sam. 10:24)

Why would we shout? Because of our loyalty to the King who rules over all.

> Make a joyful noise unto the Lord, all the earth: make a loud noise, and rejoice, and sing praise. Sing unto the Lord with the harp; with the harp, and the voice of a psalm. With trumpets and sound of cornet make a joyful noise before the Lord, the King. (Ps. 98:4–6)

Because God rules over all, the psalmist summons all nations to shout to the Lord.

Read Romans 15:8–13. Discuss how this passage fulfills the Old Testament expectation that the nations would make a joyful noise unto the Lord. How should this affect your outlook when you gather together with other believers?

_____

_____

_____

_____

_____

Worship

Psalm 100:2
Serve the Lord with gladness.

The word *serve* means *to work*. In other words, there is effort
involved in worship. For example, God commanded the Jews
to keep the Passover every year. Though it was a time of worship, it was also called service.

> And it shall come to pass, when ye be come to the
> land which the Lord will give you, according as
> he hath promised, that ye shall keep this service.
> (Ex. 12:25)

Service continues to be part of the spiritual worship of New
Testament believers, because we devote our bodies—in other
words, our entire beings—to live for God's glory.

> I beseech you therefore, brethren, by the mercies
> of God, that ye present your bodies a living sacri-
> fice, holy, acceptable unto God, which is your rea-
> sonable service [spiritual worship]. (Rom. 12:1)

We are to serve with gladness unto the Lord. This is worship!
A joyful God is glorified by joyful servants. We have to remind
ourselves that everyday tasks are part of how we serve God, and
that we can truly serve Him only with abundant joy and cheer-
fulness. Not only must we worship God joyfully when we gather
as the church, we must worship Him joyfully all the time.

In contrast, those who do not serve God with gladness eventu-
ally demonstrate that they are not His servants at all. Time and
again Israel failed to serve God with gladness and incurred His
judgment.

> Because thou servedst not the Lord thy God with
> joyfulness, and with gladness of heart, for the
> abundance of all things; therefore shalt thou serve
> thine enemies which the Lord shall send against
> thee. (Deut. 28:47–48)

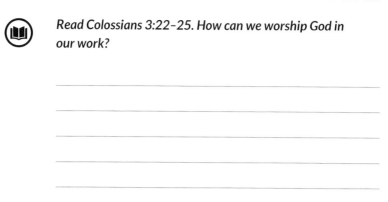

Read Colossians 3:22–25. How can we worship God in our work?

_____

_____

_____

_____

_____

Come

Psalm 100:2
Come before his presence with singing.

This parallel thought to the first phrase in verse two focuses on corporate worship. We are to gather together with loud, joyful singing to God.

> Let us come before his presence with thanks-giving, and make a joyful noise unto him with psalms. For the Lord is a great God, and a great King above all gods. (Ps. 95:2–3).

God clearly prescribes music as an aspect of worship. Therefore we should carefully weigh our musical forms in light of His nature. Specifically, is our music filled with joy? These first three commands—*shout, worship*, and *come*—are accompanied with *joy, gladness*, and *joyful singing*. God's people cannot worship Him without singing joyfully.

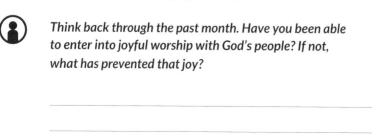

Think back through the past month. Have you been able to enter into joyful worship with God's people? If not, what has prevented that joy?

_____

_____

_____

_____

_____

Know

Psalm 100:3

Know ye that the Lord he is God: it is he that hath made us, and not we ourselves; we are his people, and the sheep of his pasture.

To know is to be intimately familiar with another person. True worship displays an experiential relationship with the only true God. His status is exclusive. He is the only one who fits the category of God. The keystone verse in ancient Israel was Deuteronomy 6:4: "Hear, O Israel: The Lord our God is one Lord."

Our God is both transcendent and immanent—far greater than we can imagine, yet much nearer than we realize. He is our Creator and our Shepherd. We are His people by creation and His sheep by redemption. In both ways God sovereignly claims us as His own.

Romans 1 teaches that humans are naturally prone to worship the creature instead of our Creator. Though most of us did not grow up with physical idols of false deities, we live in a culture drowning in idolatry. Discuss how our worship can be distorted or obstructed by idolatry. What can we do to develop the intimate familiarity with the living God that true worship requires?

Enter

Psalm 100:4

Enter into his gates with thanksgiving, and into his courts with praise.

Jerusalem was the place where the Jews were commanded to worship God. Thousands of pilgrims would ascend to the holy city in order to worship at the temple during their annual feasts. As the groups of worshipers entered into the city, they would walk through the golden gate with loud shouts of thanksgiving. As they made their way up to the Temple Mount, they would enter into its large courtyard with songs of praise.

Give Thanks and Praise

Psalm 100:4

Be thankful unto him, and bless his name.

The final two commands are simple yet clearly focused. The word *thanksgiving* is rooted in the idea of throwing or casting. We are to *throw* verbal confessions of thanksgiving on God. Though the context of this psalm is corporate worship, the New Testament emphasizes that thankful worship is our duty continually. As Paul says in 1 Thessalonians 5:18, "In everything give thanks: for this is the will of God in Christ Jesus concerning you."

> By him therefore let us offer the sacrifice of praise
> to God continually, that is, the fruit of our lips giv-
> ing thanks to his name. (Heb. 13:15)

The word *bless* in Hebrew means *to kneel down* and bless God. We bless Him—or in other words, we give Him honor—because He has blessed us. Gratitude turns to blessing. Sometimes we picture worship as unfettered emotion. As noted above, true worship certainly is joyous. But it also is infused with humble gratitude and dignified honor.

Conclusion

After exhorting us in seven different ways to praise the Lord, the psalmist concludes by telling us why we should engage in such intense worship. It is because of who He is!

Psalm 100:5

For the Lord is good.

The Lord is good! He is benevolent toward His children. He wants what is spiritually and morally best for us and blesses us with His gifts. In fact, "Every good gift and every perfect gift is from above, and cometh down from the Father of lights, with whom is no variableness, neither shadow of turning" (James 1:17).

Psalm 100:5

His mercy is everlasting.

God's mercy is His loyal covenant love. The Lord has bound Himself to us in an eternal covenant rooted in His eternal love for us and expressed through the saving work of His Son and Spirit.

Psalm 100:5

And his truth endureth to all generations.

God's truth refers to His trustworthiness. God is faithful to His promises from generation to generation. What He promised in the past He will perform in the present and for eternity!

Read Psalm 100:5 again. Think of five ways in which the Lord has demonstrated His goodness, mercy, and trustworthiness to you. Then offer a prayer of thanksgiving to Him based on these reasons, perhaps more.

_____

_____

_____

_____

_____

What does our praise for God tell us about His character and redemptive work? Write this down in your biography of God.

_____

_____

_____

_____

_____

Notes

09

PSALM 121
The Lord Is My Helper and Keeper

David Livingstone, the famous missionary and explorer of the continent of Africa, read Psalm 121 and Psalm 135, which praises God for his sovereign rule over all things, as he worshiped with his father and sister before setting out for Africa in 1840. His mother-in-law, Mrs. Moffat, wrote him at Linyardi that Psalm 121 was always in her mind as she thought about and prayed for him.[1]

Three times a year the Jewish people were required by law to make a journey to the city of Jerusalem for their annual feasts. These festivals were called Passover, Pentecost, and Tabernacles. These pilgrimages were times of worship resulting in spiritual refreshing, renewing, and rejoicing.

On their long journey, the traveling pilgrims would sing the book of Psalms, the Jewish songbook. In particular, they sang their way through Psalms 120–134. This section is known as the Psalms of Ascents.

Why this designation? Topographically, Jerusalem was the highest city in Israel (2,478 feet above sea level). Everyone who traveled there spent most of their time going up or ascending. Therefore, they were called Psalms of Ascent because pilgrims sang them on their journey up to Jerusalem.

---

[1] James Montgomery Boice, *Psalms: Psalms 107–150* (Grand Rapids: Baker Books, 2005), 3:1075.

Why did they sing these specific psalms? There was a deeper purpose than just helping weary travelers mentally endure a tough physical hike. They were instructional. They taught spiritual lessons to spiritual pilgrims as they encountered the difficult road of life. They were also inspirational. They strengthened pilgrims' knowledge and faith as they faced the struggles of the journey.

It is significant that the Israelites sang together on their annual pilgrimages. Why is sacred music an important part of the Christian life?

_____

_____

_____

_____

_____

So what can we learn from Psalm 121? Travel in ancient times was both difficult and dangerous. There were perils at every turn. The lesson this psalm is communicating to all pilgrims is that God is both our helper and keeper throughout life's journey. So what do all spiritual pilgrims encounter about God on life's journey?

The Lord Is Our Helper

Psalm 121:1–2

I will lift up mine eyes unto the hills, from whence cometh my help. My help cometh from the Lord, which made heaven and earth.

The word for *help* in Hebrew is found in Genesis 2:18 and 20 as a description for the first woman, who was created to be the helper of the first man.

> And the Lord God said, It is not good that the man should be alone; I will make him an help meet for him. . . . And Adam gave names to all cattle, and to the fowl of the air, and to every beast of the field; but for Adam there was not found an help meet for him.

The name Hebrew parents gave their child often reflected their trust in God through the experiences of life. In Exodus 18 Moses named his second son Eliezer. By naming his son Eliezer, Moses testified that God delivered him from certain death by the sword of the king of Egypt (Ex. 18:4).

The Lord is our helper. He does not abandon His children. He promises to come and assist us as a helper through the difficulties of our journey.

The opening verse of Psalm 121 poses an interpretation issue. Some English translations place a question mark at the end of the phrase: "From whence cometh my help?" The idea is that when travelers hiked from Jericho up to Jerusalem, the journey was so treacherous and dangerous that a pilgrim saw the hills and became concerned about his safety. The phrase would be a question of concern: "Where is my help in this foreboding circumstance?"

Others interpret this phrase by placing a period at the end of the sentence so that it becomes a statement of confidence. That is, "My help comes from the place (Mount Zion) where the presence of God dwells in the temple." David makes a similar statement in Psalm 20: "The name of the God of Jacob defend thee; send thee help from the sanctuary" (20:1–2).

In either case, whether it is a statement or a question, the writer's answer is clear regarding the source of his help: "My help cometh from the Lord, which made heaven and earth" (121:2). The Lord truly is our helper throughout life's journey. As Creator of the heavens and earth, He serves, supplies, and supports His children by providing all our needs.

In 1 Samuel 7 the ark of the Lord was placed in a town called Kiriath-jearim and stayed there for twenty years. During this time the Israelites drifted away from the Lord. The prophet Samuel spoke to God's people and said that if they returned to the Lord, then He would deliver them out of the hand of their enemies, the Philistines. Samuel's instructions to God's people were very clear:

- Return to the Lord with all your hearts
- Put away the idols you adopted from the heathen
- Prepare your hearts to be devoted to God's service alone.

What did they do? The people responded in humility and obedience. Samuel called for all Israel to gather at Mizpah to pray to God. When the Philistines heard that Israel was in Mizpah, they went up to battle against them. The quickly approaching enemy terrified the Israelites, and they became desperate. They told Samuel to continue in perpetual prayer to the Lord. And God did a powerful work, raining down thunder and confusion and death on the Philistines (1 Sam. 7:10)!

As a result, Samuel set up a stone to remember what God had done.

> Then Samuel took a stone, and set it between Mizpeh and Shen, and called the name of it Eben-ezer [the stone of help], saying, Hitherto hath the Lord helped us. (1 Sam. 7:12)

So in the second stanza of the great hymn, "Come, Thou Fount of Every Blessing", we sing:

Here I raise my Ebenezer;
hither by Thy help I'm come;
and I hope, by Thy good pleasure,
safely to arrive at home.[2]

Think about a difficult circumstance that you or someone you love has experienced. How was God your Helper during that time?

_____

_____

_____

_____

_____

The Lord Is Our Keeper

The Hebrew word translated *keep* or *preserve* is used six times in these six verses to describe our God. It means He watches over us. "It was used to describe a gardener tending his garden (Gen. 2:15), a shepherd watching over his flock (Gen. 30:31), and a man watching over a house (Ecc. 12:3)."[3] It conveys the idea of caring for and guarding something, like a soccer goalie who guards his goal from the opposing team. God is our keeper in three ways as we journey through life.

---

[2]Robert Robinson, "Come, Thou Fount of Every Blessing," 1758.
[3]Lawson, *Holman Old Testament Commentary—Psalms 76–150*, 268.

He Keeps Us from Falling Under the Heavy Weight of the Journey

Psalm 121:3

He will not suffer thy foot to be moved.

Ancient travelers carried their luggage, and at times the weight was too much. Regardless of how heavy our burdens, we can roll them onto the Lord.

> Cast thy burden upon the Lord, and he shall sustain thee: he shall never suffer the righteous to be moved. (Ps. 55:22)

 When we think of the Lord's help, physical safety and provision often come to mind first. But what about our hearts? What about the need to persevere in faith? We easily get weary in our spiritual journey. Read verse 24 of Jude and describe the comfort it provides.

_____

_____

_____

_____

He Cares for Us Constantly

Psalm 121:3–4

He that keepeth thee will not slumber. Behold, he that keepeth Israel shall neither slumber nor sleep.

God is never distracted or disinterested in our journey. He never takes a break for a nap because He is tired. When we sleep, He is awake and alert. His strength is always infinite. We experience unforeseen circumstances. We often talk about events that are outside of our control. Surprise and inability are two situations God has never experienced. We can take refuge in His constant care.

He Protects Us from Imminent Danger

Psalm 121:5–8

The Lord is thy keeper: the Lord is thy shade upon thy right hand. The sun shall not smite thee by day, nor the moon by night. The Lord shall preserve thee from all evil: he shall preserve thy soul. The Lord shall preserve thy going out and thy coming in from this time forth, and even for evermore.

The sun is oppressively hot in the Judean wilderness. The relentless heat drains the traveler of his strength, and heat stroke is an ever-present danger. A place of shade is a welcome comfort and relief. The psalmist is affirming that God provides comfort and relief from life's heat.

The moon reminds us of the dangers that hide in the shadow and lurk in the darkness. Likewise, God is always there to protect us from all harm physically or spiritually.

In other words, the Lord is our helper and our keeper throughout the entire journey of life. God was with the pilgrims night and day as they went to Jerusalem and as they made their way home. God will be with us, His children, until we safely arrive to our heavenly home.

 The New Testament describes the Holy Spirit as our helper. Look up the following verses: John 15:26; John 16:7; Romans 8:26. List the ways in which the Holy Spirit is our helper. Add these to your biography of God.

_____

_____

_____

Prayer: Dear Lord, I look to You to be my helper and my keeper. Thank You that You have promised to provide my every need and to protect me along my journey. Keep me from evil and temptation. I depend on You for the power to overcome my own nature. I roll the burdens I am carrying on You. I ask for Your continual presence to bring me relief and comfort. Thank You that Your power is eternal and Your care is perpetual.

Notes

10

PSALM 139
Lead Me in the Everlasting Way

The reflections of the past and the present situation
express a profound knowledge of God and a conviction
that this God has a concern for individuals.
Yahweh loves and knows his people, and they,
in turn, need not be afraid of his scrutiny.[1]

How intimate are your thoughts about God? Are they as intimate as God's thoughts about you? That would be impossible.

In Psalm 139 King David writes a compelling description of an infinite, immense God who is intimately aware of every person in the world. The purpose of this description is to overwhelm each one of us with the mind-blowing reality that God knows everything about us. As a result of this knowledge, we should be willing for God to identify anything that is grievous to Him in order that we may forsake it and walk in His ways.

Psalm 139 is a lesson in practical theology. David is not writing in the abstract. He takes the highest doctrinal truths about the nature of God and brings them down to where we personally live. He writes to both the head and the heart. So behold your God and stand in awe!

---

[1]VanGemeren, 5:835.

What Does God Know?

Psalm 139:1
O Lord, thou hast searched me, and known me.

Like a mining company looking for gold, God has searched deep into our hearts and minds. He is intimately and thoroughly acquainted with us. He knows everything about us— inside and out! He knows us better than we know ourselves. God is omniscient.

Psalm 139:2
Thou knowest my downsitting and mine uprising, thou understandest my thought afar off.

God knows us like no one else. He sees us when we get up in the morning to go to class. He watches us when we go to bed at night. He also knows everything that has happened during our day. God can read our minds. He knows what motivates and controls our thinking. He even knows where our thinking will end up.

Psalm 139:3
Thou compassest my path and my lying down, and art acquainted with all my ways.

Compassest literally means *to winnow*, like separating the wheat from the chaff. God carefully scrutinizes the roads we are traveling, whether we are going the right way or not. God knows when we lie down. God is thoroughly acquainted with our habits and patterns of behavior, and even secret actions.

Psalm 139:4
For there is not a word in my tongue, but, lo, O Lord, thou knowest it altogether.

God already knows what we are going to say before it comes out of our mouths because God knows the words as they are forming in our minds. This is a shocking reality to contemplate! God is intimately acquainted with every word we speak.

Psalm 139:5

Thou hast beset me behind and before, and laid thine hand upon me.

Like a city surrounded by its enemy and under siege with no place to escape, God is all around us. He is always behind us and always in front of us. Everywhere we go, God is. He has laid His hand upon us so that even if we wanted to try to escape His presence, we could not. Who can hide from God?

Psalm 139:6

Such knowledge is too wonderful for me; it is high, I cannot attain unto it.

God's omniscience is incredible, fantastic, mysterious, and incomprehensible. We worship a God that we cannot understand, and that is a good thing.

> O the depth of the riches both of the wisdom and knowledge of God! how unsearchable are his judgments, and his ways past finding out! (Rom. 11:33)

Read Romans 11:33–36. How does this passage relate to what David says about the knowledge of God in Psalm 139? Why should we be thankful we have a God whose knowledge surpasses human comprehension?

Where Is God Found?

Psalm 139:7

Whither shall I go from thy spirit? or whither shall I flee from thy presence?

The answer to David's two rhetorical questions is that it is impossible to travel somewhere to avoid God's presence. If we try to run from God, we will discover that God is already where we are headed. God is omnipresent.

Psalm 139:8–10

If I ascend up into heaven, thou art there: if I make my bed in hell, behold, thou art there. If I take the wings of the morning, and dwell in the uttermost parts of the sea; even there shall thy hand lead me, and thy right hand shall hold me.

David then answers three hypothetical questions concerning God's presence in extreme places: heaven, hell, and the ends of the universe.

If we could go up to heaven, we would find out that God is there. If we made our beds in the depths of the underworld, God would be there. If we could take wings and fly with the speed of light to the corners of the universe, God would always be there to guide us and protect us by His own power.

Psalm 139:11–12

If I say, Surely the darkness shall cover me; even the night shall be light about me. Yea, the darkness hideth not from thee; but the night shineth as the day: the darkness and the light are both alike to thee.

95

While many people try to hide in the dark, David knew that darkness does not affect God's vision. The darkness is not darkness to God. "Dark times are light to God. He is present in them, knowing perfectly all that is transpiring and what his eternal purposes are."[2]

What Can God Do?

Psalm 139:13

For thou hast possessed my reins: thou hast covered me in my mother's womb.

David then explains his awe of God's omnipotence demonstrated in creation. He acknowledges that God created his inward parts. Specifically, the word *reins* refers to the kidneys. It symbolizes the inner parts and seat of one's emotions. While David was in his mother's womb, he was skillfully woven and knitted together by God. It is clear from this section that David was a human being at conception.

Psalm 139:14

I will praise thee; for I am fearfully and wonderfully made: marvellous are thy works; and that my soul knoweth right well.

David understands that God's formation of him in his mother's womb is "wonderful." That means that God does what no human could ever do—create another human being. David confesses that God is wonderful (Isa. 9:6) and worships Him with reverential awe.

---

[2]Lawson, *Holman Old Testament Commentary–Psalms 76–150*, 334.

Psalm 139:15

My substance was not hid from thee, when I was made in secret, and curiously wrought in the lowest parts of the earth.

David had mentioned his inner organs being created by God. Now he speaks of his skeletal frame—"my substance"—being intricately woven and fashioned in secret and in the lowest parts of the earth (two metaphors referring to his mother's womb).

"Embroidered with great skill"[3] is an accurate poetical description of the creation of veins, sinews, muscles, nerves, etc. What tapestry can equal the human fabric?

Psalm 139:16

Thine eyes did see my substance, yet being unperfect; and in thy book all my members were written, which in continuance were fashioned [what days they should be fashioned], when as yet there was none of them.

David describes God's seeing him as an unformed embryo: "my substance, yet being unperfect." In that condition before there was ever a conception, God had already written in His book all the days that David would live on this earth including when he was born, how long he would live, when he would die, and what he would accomplish. Jeremiah says the same thing about his life:

> Before I formed thee in the belly I knew thee; and before thou camest forth out of the womb I sanctified thee, and I ordained thee a prophet unto the nations. (Jer. 1:5)

Like a potter forms the clay in his hands, our entire lives are shaped by God's sovereign hands.

---

[3]Spurgeon, 7:226.

Psalm 139:13–16 persuasively speak of the personal dignity of an unborn human being. Discuss the truths declared in David's statements.

Psalm 139:17–18

How precious also are thy thoughts unto me, O God! how great is the sum of them! If I should count them, they are more in number than the sand: when I awake, I am still with thee.

David acknowledges the value of these kinds of thoughts. What security and comfort this brings to every believer who knows that God is in control of his life! David also acknowledges that these thoughts flooded his mind in such a vast way that even if he tried to count them, they would be like numbering the grains of sand on the seashore. These innumerable thoughts about God absorbed David's thinking and sustained him day after day.

How Should We Respond?

So how should we respond to what we have encountered in this psalm concerning God's omniscience, omnipresence, and omnipotence?

We Should Reject the Way of Evil

Psalm 139:19–22

Surely thou wilt slay the wicked, O God: depart from me therefore, ye bloody men. For they speak against thee wickedly, and thine enemies take thy name in vain. Do not I hate them, O Lord, that hate thee? and am not I grieved with those that rise up against thee? I hate them with perfect hatred: I count them mine enemies.

The character of God that David has described so amazingly in these verses is the primary reason David reacts so abruptly to those who are God's enemies. These words seem harsh and reactionary until we learn to think like David.

These men are described as wicked, murderous, enemies, and haters of God. They speak maliciously, blasphemously, and rebelliously against God. David's response is consistent with God's response. If they hate God, David hates them. If they are God's enemies, they are David's enemies. David draws a sharp dividing line between him and those who are intent on evil.

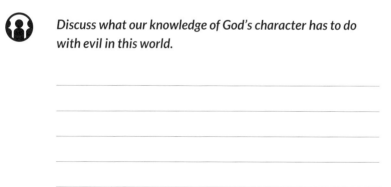

Discuss what our knowledge of God's character has to do with evil in this world.

_____

_____

_____

_____

_____

We Should Walk in God's Way

Psalm 139:23–24

Search me, O God, and know my heart: try me, and know my thoughts: and see if there be any wicked way in me, and lead me in the way everlasting.

David knew all too well the sinfulness of his own heart. Though he hated sin he was still prone to wander. Therefore he was not just hard on his enemies, he was hard on himself!

David goes back to the beginning. He eagerly makes a request to God based on what God revealed about Himself in verse one. He opens himself up to God in complete transparency. He asks God to investigate him and be intimately acquainted with his soul and his thoughts. He asked God to perceive if there is anything in him that would cause pain or grief to God, himself, or others. David wanted to be in a place where he could confess and forsake his sins (Ps. 51).

He concludes with the desire to be led in the "way everlasting." Since David came from God, he wanted to go back to God. This is the spirit of any true believer, even though we struggle mightily with sin and feel impure in the presence of a holy God. "Christians don't want God to leave them alone."[4]

Does God's all-knowing presence comfort or frighten you? Why? If His omniscience is terrifying, perhaps there is sin that He wants to purge from your heart. Remember, He is a good Shepherd whose knowledge of His sheep is not just omniscient but redeeming and secure (John 10:14).

---

[4] Aaron Coffey, BJU evangelistic service, January 15, 2015.

Review Psalm 139 and fill out your biography of God. What is it about the characteristics David mentions that grabs your attention?

_____

_____

_____

_____

_____

Prayer: O Lord, You know everything about me. You are everywhere before I get there. You have known the specifics of my tomorrow since before time began. Search me. Discern my thoughts. Show me where I need to change. Purge the evil from my soul. Help me to take refuge in You alone. Reign over me, for You not only are all-knowing and all-present, You are always good. I want to trust You with all my heart. Amen.

Notes

11

PSALM 150
Hallelujah!

The note of praise swells out more and more strongly toward the close of the book, finally to break out in this crescendo which is full-toned and jubilant.[1]

The book of Psalms begins with a promise, "Blessed is . . ." (1:1), and ends with a praise, "Praise ye the Lord" (150:6). In between the first and last psalms, we learn about the life that encounters God. What does one say at the end of a life that has known God and walked with Him? Praise the Lord!

Psalm 150 is a climatic conclusion to a collection of five praise Psalms (146–150) where everyone and everything are to praise God everywhere. This psalm speaks of the ultimate end of a life that has encountered God. This final psalm presents the basic questions and sets forth the biblical pattern of praise.

---

[1] H. C. Leupold, *Exposition of the Psalms* (Grand Rapids: Baker Publishing House, 1970), 1005.

What Does It Mean to Praise God?

Psalm 150:1

Praise ye the LORD.

The Hebrew for "Praise ye the Lord" is *hallelujah*. *Hallel* means *to praise*; *Jah* is the shortened form of the word for the Lord. So you can read it: *Hallel-u-Jah. You praise the Lord!*

Praise is like light radiating from the sun. It conveys the idea of cheering, shouting, and clapping, like at the conclusion of a great concert. It often means to boast or brag about something someone has done. *To praise* is *to extol enthusiastically the greatness of someone or something with words of excellence.*

We are commanded to praise the Lord thirteen times in these six verses. Praising God is not an option; it is an obligation. It is both our delight and our duty. The greatest truth about God is that He is worthy of our praise, and the deepest truth about ourselves is that we have been created to praise Him.

What does it mean to praise God? It is expressing joyful delight in His divine presence. When we do this, we realize the ultimate purpose of our existence.

 Why is praising God **the ultimate purpose of our existence?**

_____

_____

_____

_____

_____

Where Do We Praise God?

Psalm 150:1

Praise God in his sanctuary.

In the Old Testament the Jewish people were commanded to praise God by going up to Jerusalem and worshiping Him in His holy temple or sanctuary.

> Enter into his gates with thanksgiving, and into his courts with praise. (Ps. 100:4)

Today the Lord's presence dwells inside every believer (1 Cor. 3:16; 6:19) and in the corporate assembly of the church, the body of Christ, when we gather together for worship. We are called to worship God on earth as we meet with His chosen people.

Psalm 150:1

Praise him in the firmament of his power.

God is also to be praised in the vast expanse of heaven—"the firmament of his power." All of heaven is a display of God's infinite power and wisdom. As Psalm 19:1 states, "The heavens declare the glory of God; and the firmament showeth his handywork." This kind of awesome display means heaven is a place of praise. Heaven and earth are to be a unified choir of praise.

> Praise ye the Lord. Praise ye the Lord from the heavens: praise him in the heights. Praise ye him, all his angels: praise ye him, all his hosts. (Ps. 148:1–2)

Where do we praise God? Everywhere! If there is no space that does not declare God's glory, there is no place where His image bearers should not proclaim His praise.

Why Do We Praise God?

Psalm 150:2

Praise him for his mighty acts:

We are to praise God for what He does. He displays His strength and saving might. For example, Daniel praised God because he understood that his ability to interpret king Nebuchadnezzar's secret dream was due to God's wisdom and might (Dan. 2:20).

God's mighty acts are revealed especially when He rescues and delivers His own people through prayer. David testifies, "Now know I that the Lord saveth his anointed; he will hear him from his holy heaven with the saving strength of his right hand" (Ps. 20:6). Successive generations are called to praise God for His mighty acts.

> One generation shall praise thy works to another,
> and shall declare thy mighty acts. (Ps. 145:4)

Read Ephesians 1:3–14 and note the phrase "unto the praise of . . ." What mighty acts of God is Paul declaring are praiseworthy?

Psalm 150:2

Praise him according to his excellent greatness.

We are also to praise God for Who He is. *Excellent* refers to abundance. *Greatness* speaks of the magnitude and majesty of

God's glorious attributes like faithfulness, mercy, grace, love, righteousness, holiness, justice, and wisdom.

> O Lord God, thou hast begun to shew thy servant
> thy greatness, and thy mighty hand: for what God
> is there in heaven or in earth, that can do accord-
> ing to thy works, and according to thy might?
> (Deut. 3:24)

Why do we praise God? Because of what He does and who He is.

How Do We Praise God?

Psalm 150:4–5

*Praise him with the timbrel and dance: praise him with
stringed instruments and organs. Praise him upon the loud
cymbals: praise him upon the high sounding cymbals.*

Verses 4 and 5 of Psalm 150 describe the various musical instruments used in the temple worship by the Levitical priests.
The meaning of the word *psalm* refers to a song of praise accompanied by a stringed instrument like a harp. Psalms are
songs to praise God along with musical accompaniment.

> Instruments as accompaniments to praise, or any
> aspect of prayer for that matter, are God's will as
> His Scripture frequently shows. David led in or-
> ganizing musical ministry (1 Chr. 22–29), and it
> exercised a strategic role under the guidance of
> several later kings. It also was sorely missed in
> the exile (Ps. 137), and important under Ezra and
> Nehemiah, in the inter-testament era, and among
> New Testament believers. So it has usually had a
> stimulating ministry ever since. And heaven is

filled with music as the book of Revelation re-flects.[2]

The psalm mentions many instruments to be played either individually or in a priestly symphony in praise to God.

First, there were wind instruments, such as the trumpet. This ram's horn (shofar) was used on special occasions like in 2 Samuel 6:15: "So David and all the house of Israel brought up the ark of the Lord with shouting, and with the sound of the trumpet." The psalm also mentions "organs," which are piped instruments like the flute or pennywhistle.

Second, this praise includes stringed instruments. The psaltery was a portable instrument like a lute or guitar with ten strings (Ps. 33:2). The psalm also mentions a harp, like the instrument David played before Saul (1 Sam. 16:16, 23), as well as other stringed instruments (Ps. 150:4). The harp along with the pipe are the earliest instruments mentioned in Scripture.

> And his brother's name was Jubal: he was the father of all such as handle the harp and organ. (Gen. 4:21)

A third and final category are percussive instruments. The timbrel is like our tambourine and is linked to dancing as an expression of joy. The loud cymbals and high-sounding cymbals noted in verse five may refer to smaller cymbals like a castanet and the large, crashing cymbals used in orchestras today.

Worship in the temple was not always quiet or subdued, nor was it ever for the purpose of entertainment. It was always to be directed to the audience of one. We sing for God's glory alone!

---

[2]James E. Rosscup, *An Exposition on Prayer in the Bible: Igniting the Fuel to Flame Our Communication With God* (Chattanooga: AMG Publishers, 2011), 961-962.

Who Is to Praise God?

Psalm 150:6

Let everything that hath breath praise the Lord. Praise ye the Lord.

God is to be praised everywhere we are, because of everything He is and with everything we have by everyone and everything.

We finish where we started. A happy man (Ps. 1) is one who meditates on God's Word and follows God's way. Throughout his life he encounters God through his experiences and grows in the knowledge of God. His days should be filled with praise and should end with a hallelujah.

> By him therefore let us offer the sacrifice of praise to God continually, that is, the fruit of our lips giving thanks to his name. (Heb. 13:15)

The writer of Hebrews records words from Psalm 22 that pointed ahead to Jesus Christ Himself: "I will declare thy name unto my brethren, in the midst of the church will I sing praise unto thee" (Heb. 2:12). In other words, the Lord Himself will sing His Father's praise in the midst of the redeemed community in glory. If Christ will sing the praise of God the Father, surely we should too!

This psalm is noisy and loud. There are times in worship when we should quietly reflect before the Lord in stillness and rest. There are also times when our hearts are broken over circumstances of sin, and we should weep before the Lord in heartbroken sorrow as we cast our cares upon Him.

Then there are times when we should celebrate. We should enter into the presence of heaven with a shout! We should be praising the Lord all the time.

> From the rising of the sun unto the going down of the same the Lord's name is to be praised. (Ps. 113:3)

Do you engage your heart and voice in gathered worship? What truths about God's character or redemptive acts could you meditate on in order to glorify God with His people this week? Use these thoughts to finish your biography of God. Review what you have written and turn it into a prayer.

_____

_____

_____

_____

_____

Prayer: O Lord, thank You for shaping my heart to know and love You. Thank You for revealing Yourself to me through these psalms. Thank You for directing people to record their encounters with You in a perfect way. Thank You for showing me how Your character and works stabilized and convicted and amazed and rejoiced their souls. Thank You for giving me light for my path (Ps. 119:105).

Notes